# High Shelf

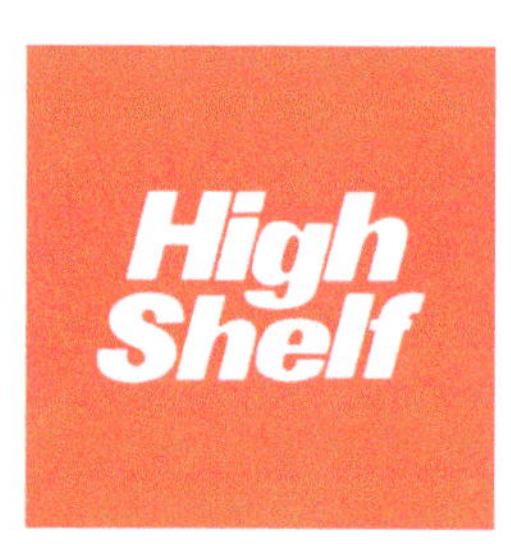

***High Shelf Issue XVII, April 2020***
Portland, Oregon.
Copyright 2020, High Shelf Press

ISBN: 978-1-7342842-8-7

Cover Image by V. B. Borjen
Design and Layout by C. M. Tollefson
Edited by David Seung & C. M. Tollefson

High Shelf Press reserves all rights to the material contained herein for the contributors protection; upon publication, all rights revert to the artists.

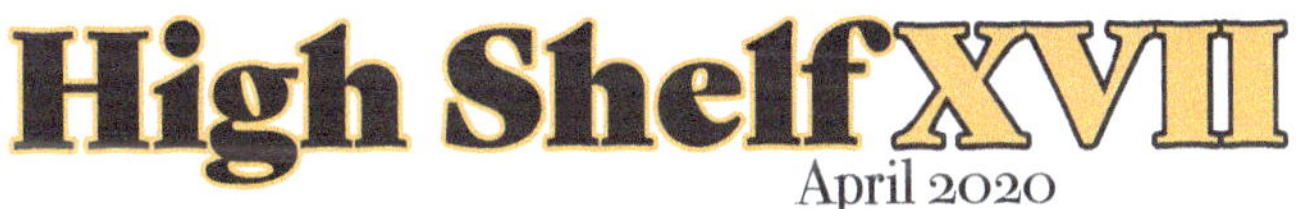


High Shelf XVII
April 2020

"There is always already a war going on

all our dead
all our little deaths

A lead heart exposed
as a chaff of grain packed in flesh..."
*Valyntina Grenier*

"...I went on huffing salt as if trying to wake from a dream,
staring over the sapphire expanse of the Atlantic,
wondering how such darkness could mirror the stars... "
*Corbin Wamble*

# Table Of Contents

# Fillioque

*Joseph Zenoni*

The rain freezes when it lands
and slick fire-lizards sprout from logs
when thrown into the stove. Our house
owns a draught I have not felt before,
which has inveigled itself into every corner,
generating blights in the flour.
Cats shame me with their fidelity,
prostrating themselves,
moving modestly, trusting their own motives.
Divorce holds no contradiction to them.
I play our father, fill the day quietly.
I cut nibs then re-sharpen my knife.
I have seen you everywhere: in petal's pattern,
and in the unfurling soot-black standards
of the gunsmoke clouds which separate us.
I've heard you in wind rushing through horizon's gap,
where heaven's dome, a jagged gash
freshly sawn by toothed treetops,
rises from this animal earth.

But it vouchsafes nothing, this north-wind's sting,
and I woke to a weasel hollering,
leg caught in the rabbit snare.
I have missed mass again.
I sat at the window and waited
until the bright boy came to make his fine points,
that not a union is a union in half,
that to divide is to be divided,
and that which cannot die is not a man.
*Brother*, I said, *take up your turban.*
*It is less than a mystery to me,*
I told him, *I'm empty, unstuck.*
I told him, *I'm opened like a puzzle-box.*
*I'm no longer committed to the truth.*
It was humiliating. A large bat

has taken up our eaves to roost,
escaping from a sky arrayed
in thunderous hoops and bights of lightning
which no pillar built can ever hope to breach.
I'm soaked to the hilt by the rain's reach.
White birches quiver.
Crows moan in the late morning freeze.

# SCORE SUSTENANCE

*Valyntina Grenier*

There is always already a war going on

all our dead
all our little deaths

A lead heart exposed
as a chaff of grain packed in flesh

In the wake of two atomic blasts
an unknown number of hearts were made ash

The almost instantaneous expansion
*violence as air*

Mortals projectile
Waves incinerate

Here we are from a page
hanging in air

Have you heard
bombs going off

Shells scatter

In a spray of shrapnel
flesh becomes mist

Bones give off carbon 13

While for you

for me
*our breath becomes mist*
for all
for each one

gather

# HOW WRONG

Sara McCall

to think we might be awarded
any completion in life—to ask if
all this chasing ends.
As if the spinning parts stop and fall.

On thicker days time passes
slow enough to see myself—

a hot tongue throbbing
in the cheek
of a damned dog
running toward nothing
waiting for a choke

# High Tea

*April Rubasch*

After the mastectomy, my uncle said they were smooth as the underside
of a frog. Said it like we were sitting over beer in a husky pub, our
profiles silhouetted by bar lamps overhung—but it was just our couch
and my parents were there and he was talking to them and not me, drunk
on choking back snot and tears—and so looking at a child, who looks
intently back. She was a stoic. The walls of her face mortared, held.
Shoulder blades jutted aerodynamically from her body. Her pinched
posture was a cottoned nosebleed. I searched the room for something to
stare at, settling on the tile cracks while the grown-ups talked and ate
small sandwiches and petit fours. When it was over, we tossed them a
slight wave from the door frame. Smiling, like good Samaritans, proud of
our kindness.

# Enter the Quiet

V. B. Borjen

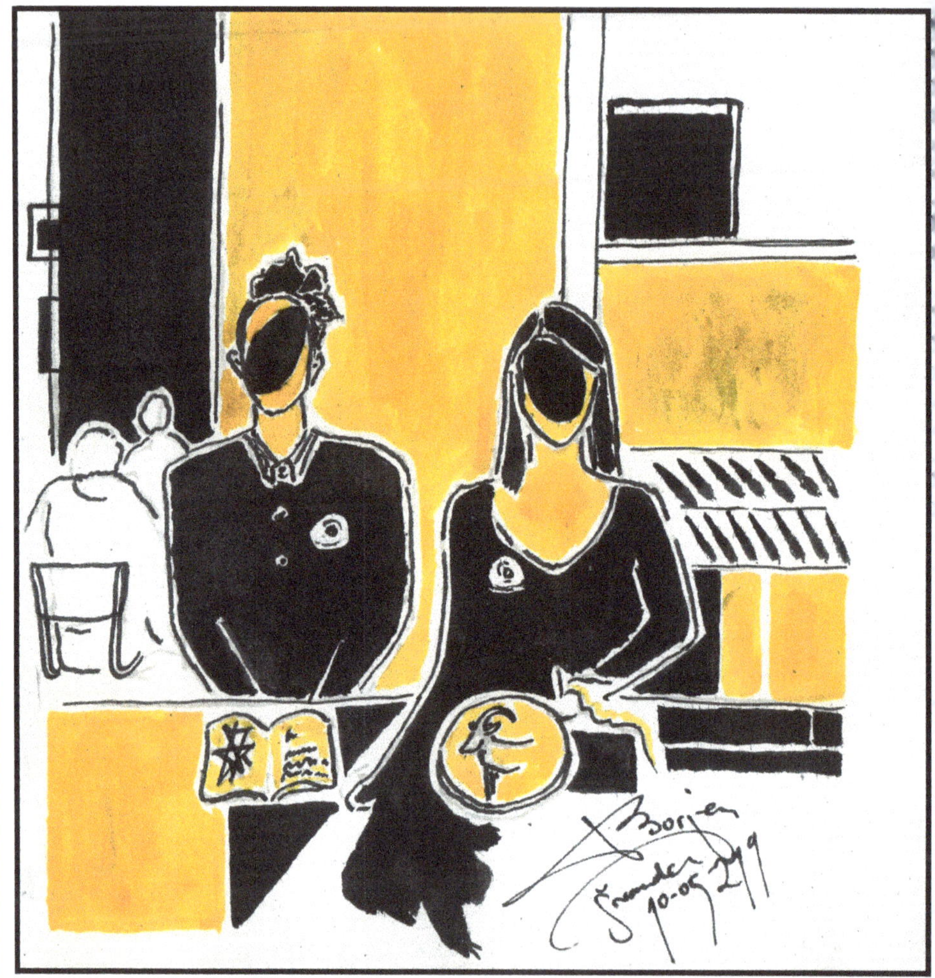

The Third Law of Thermodynamics, or Falling into Art

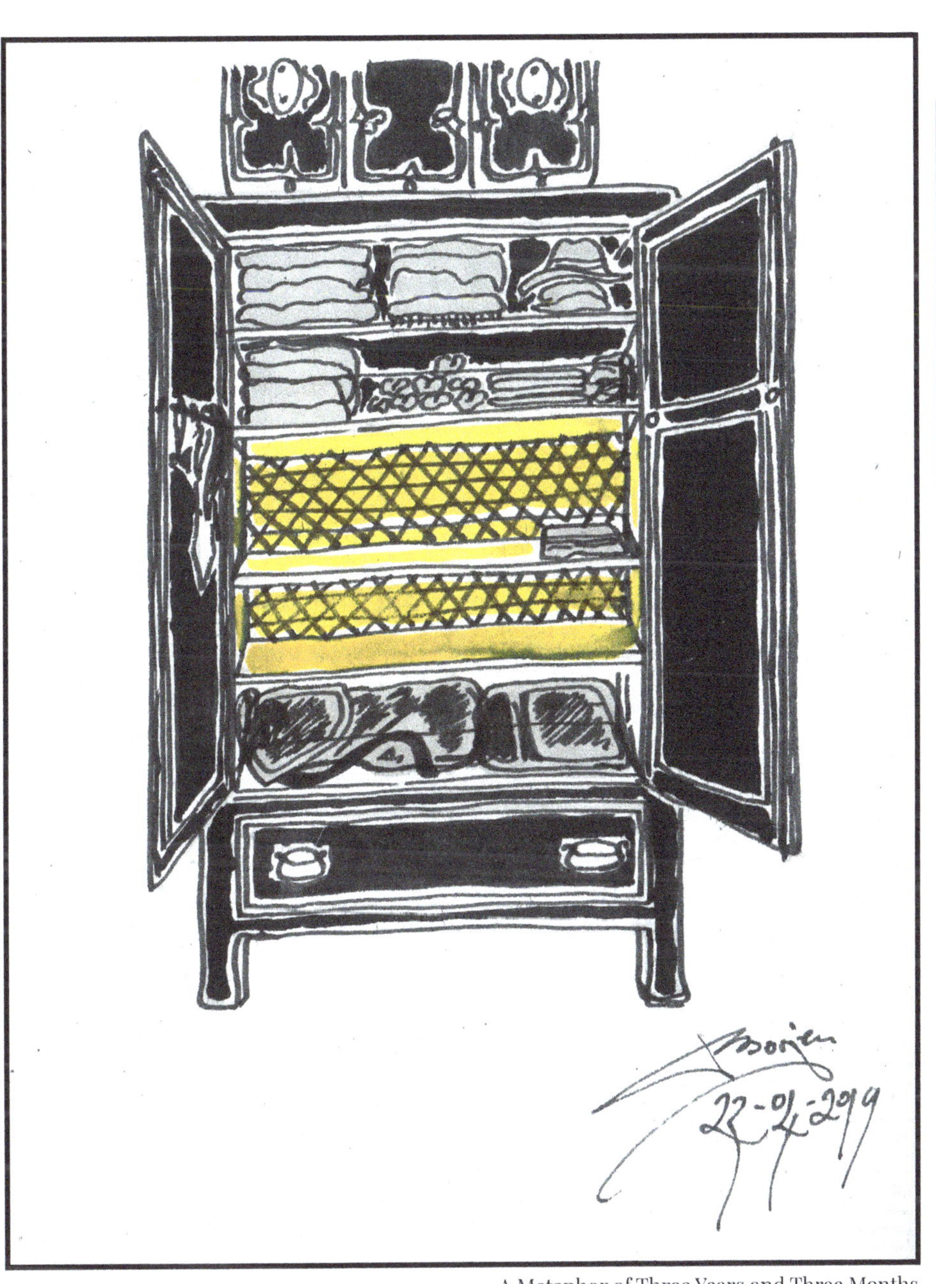

A Metaphor of Three Years and Three Months

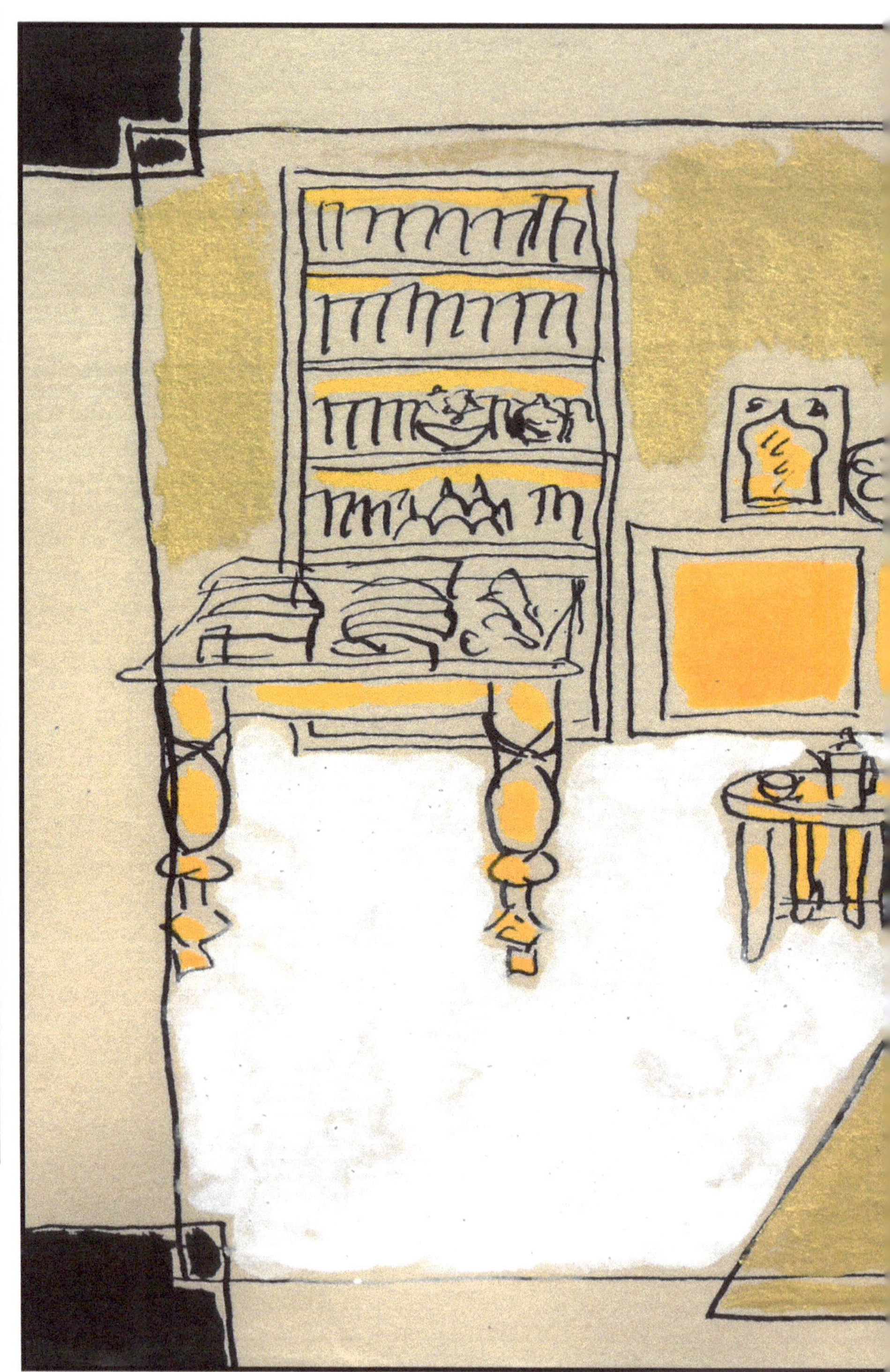

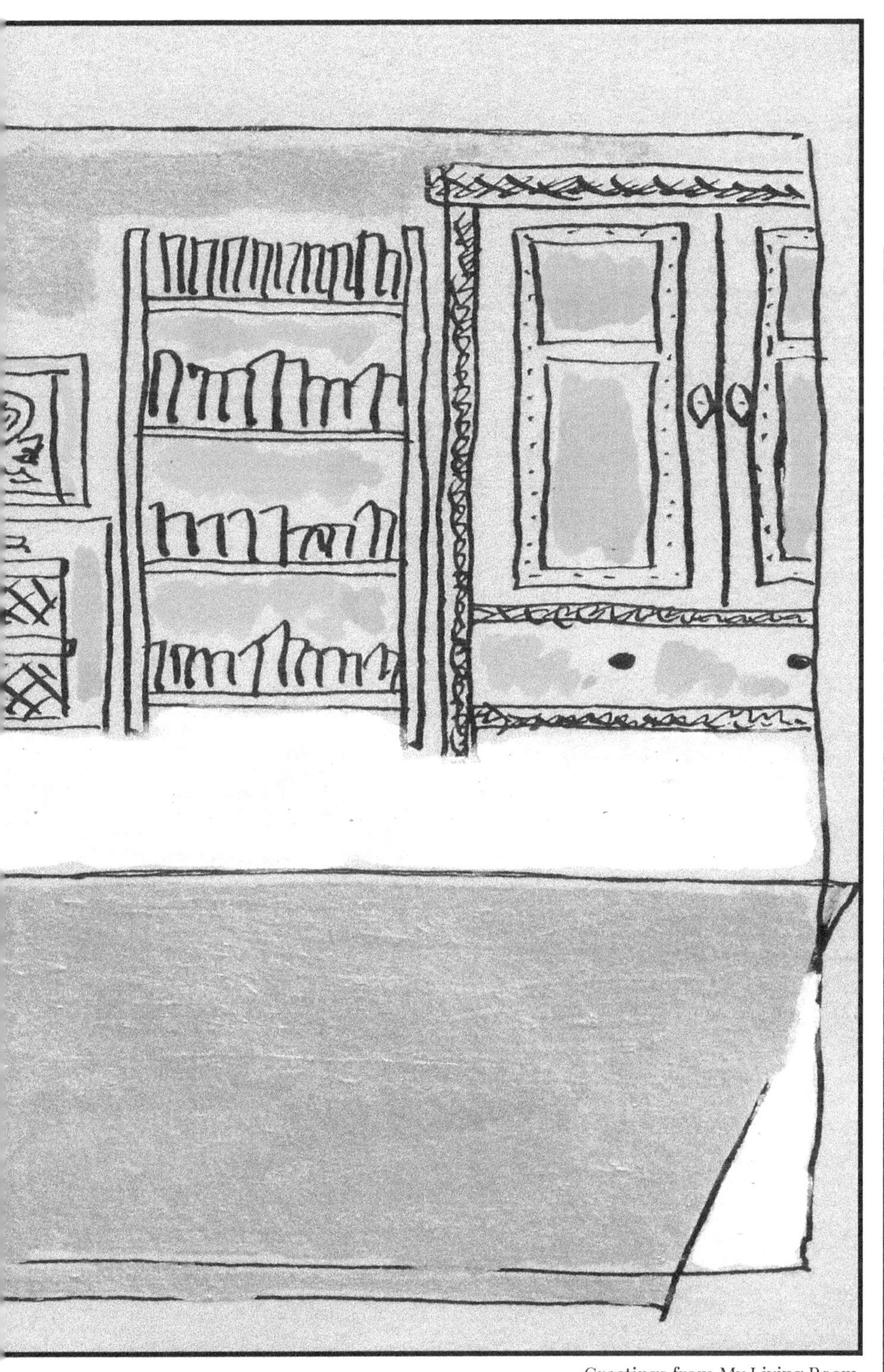

Greetings from My Living Room

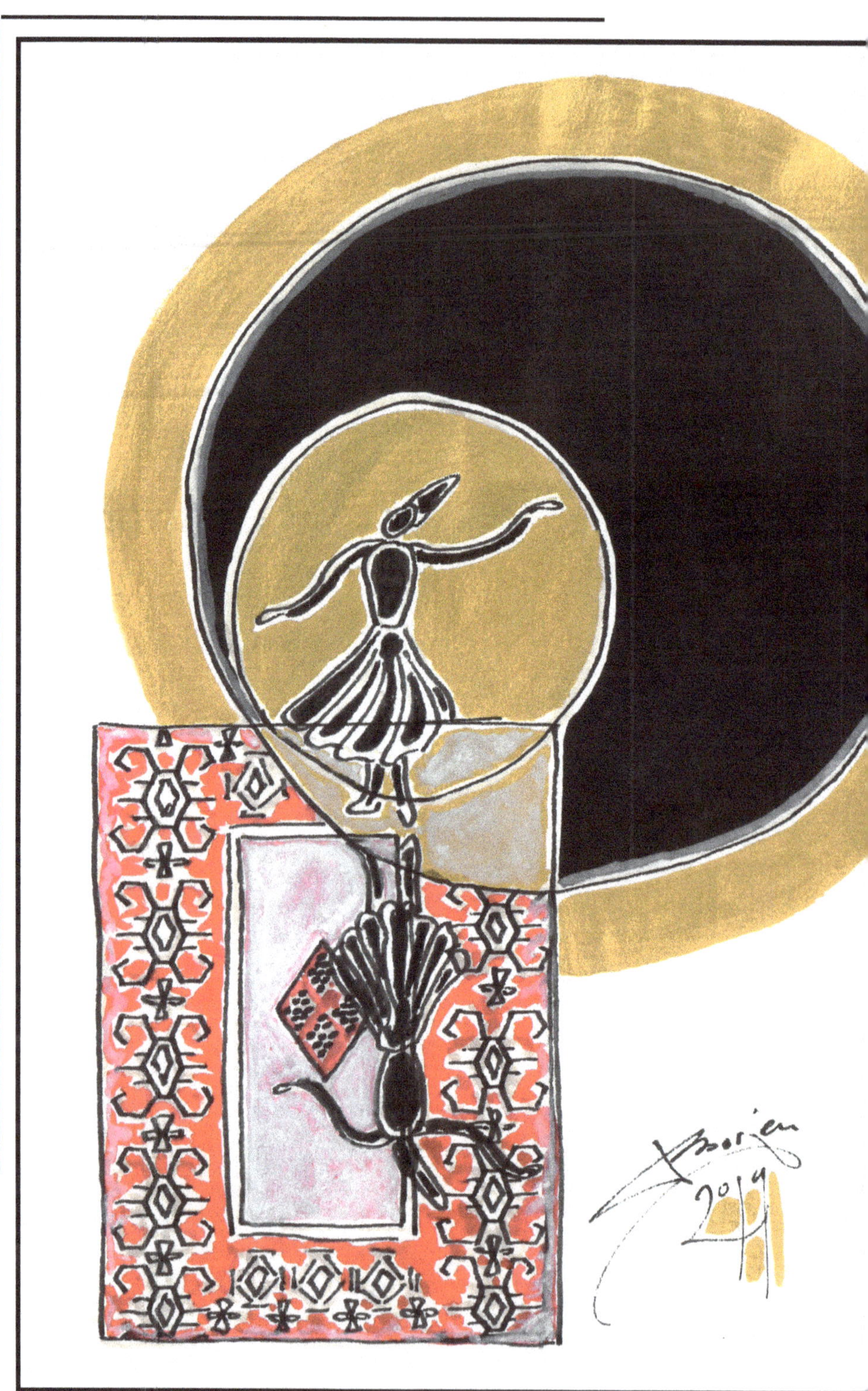

Whirl, Whirl, Whirl

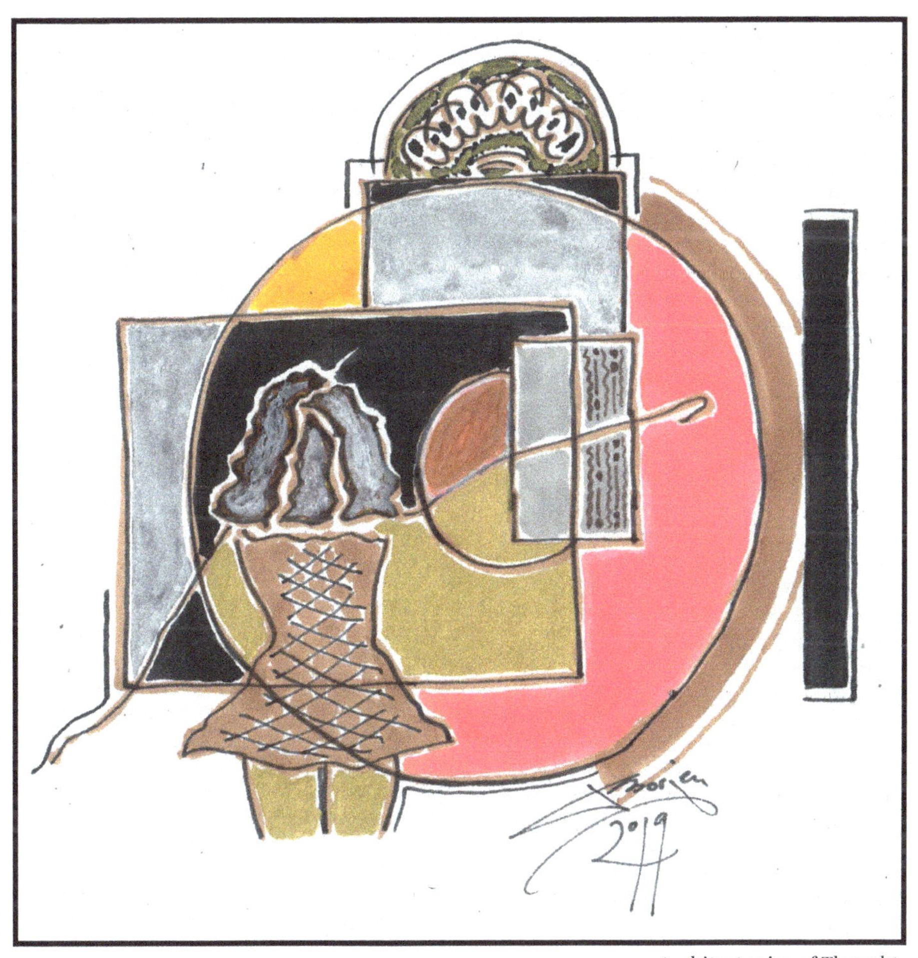

Architectonics of Thought

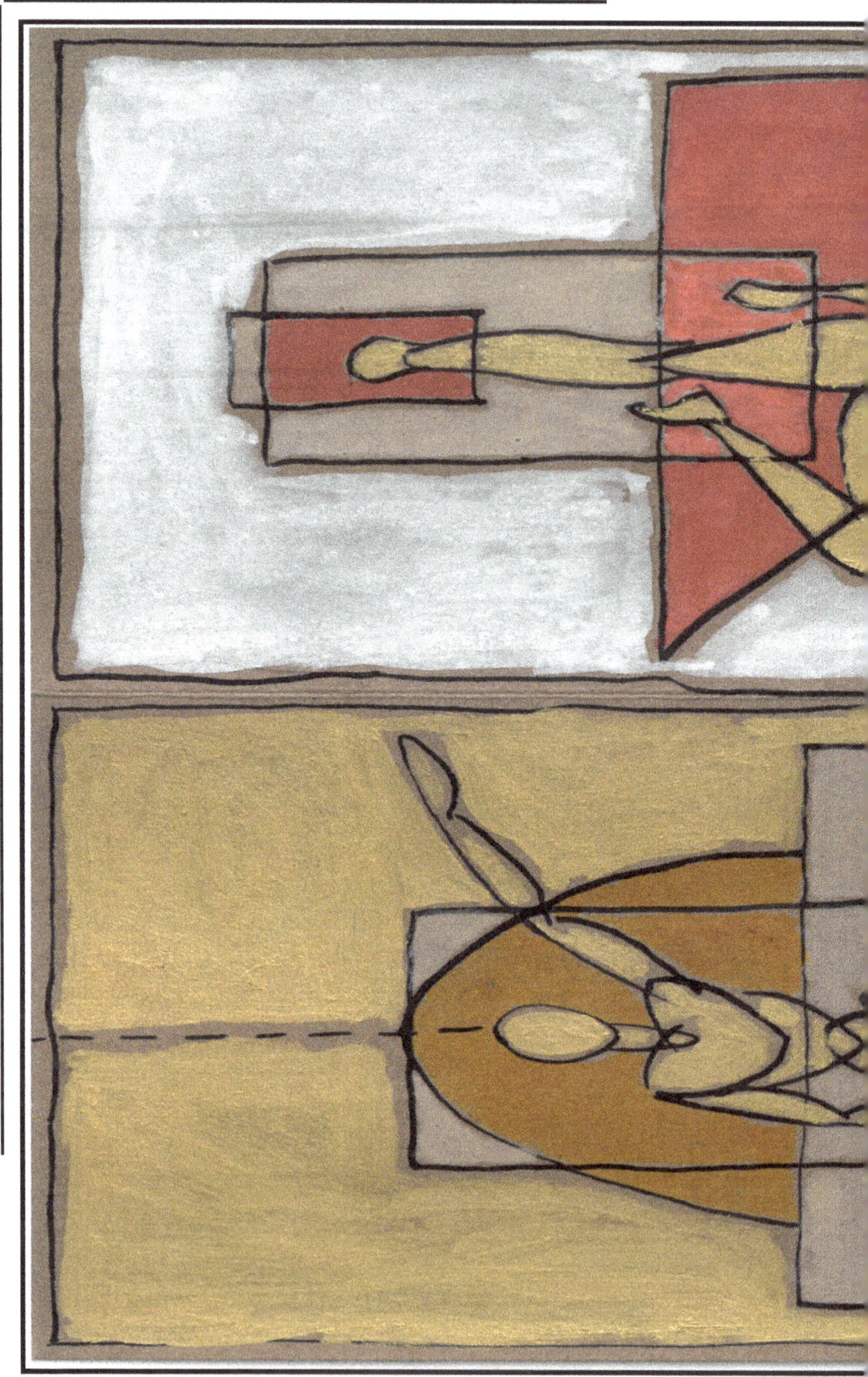

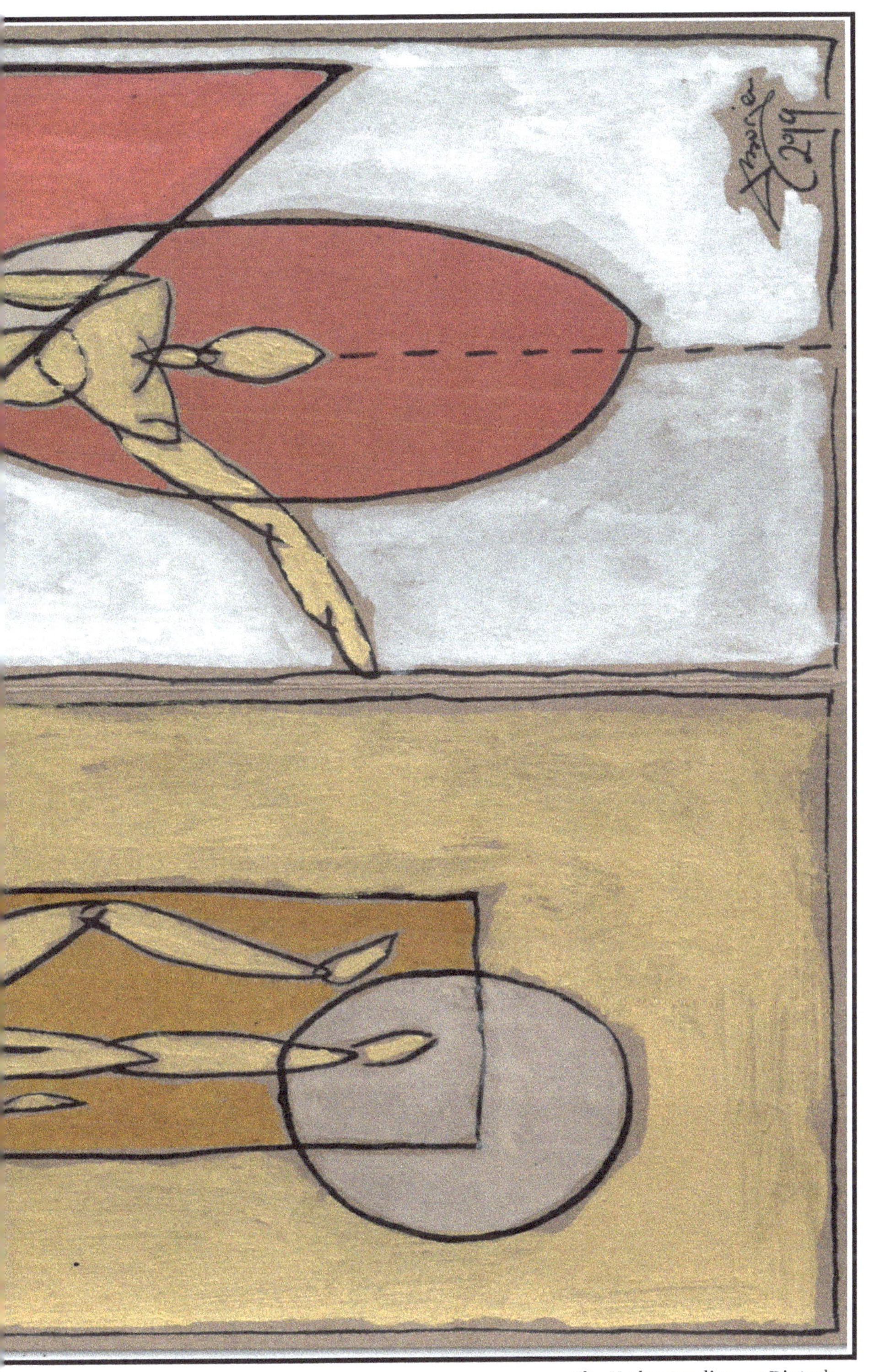

The Understanding, or Diptych

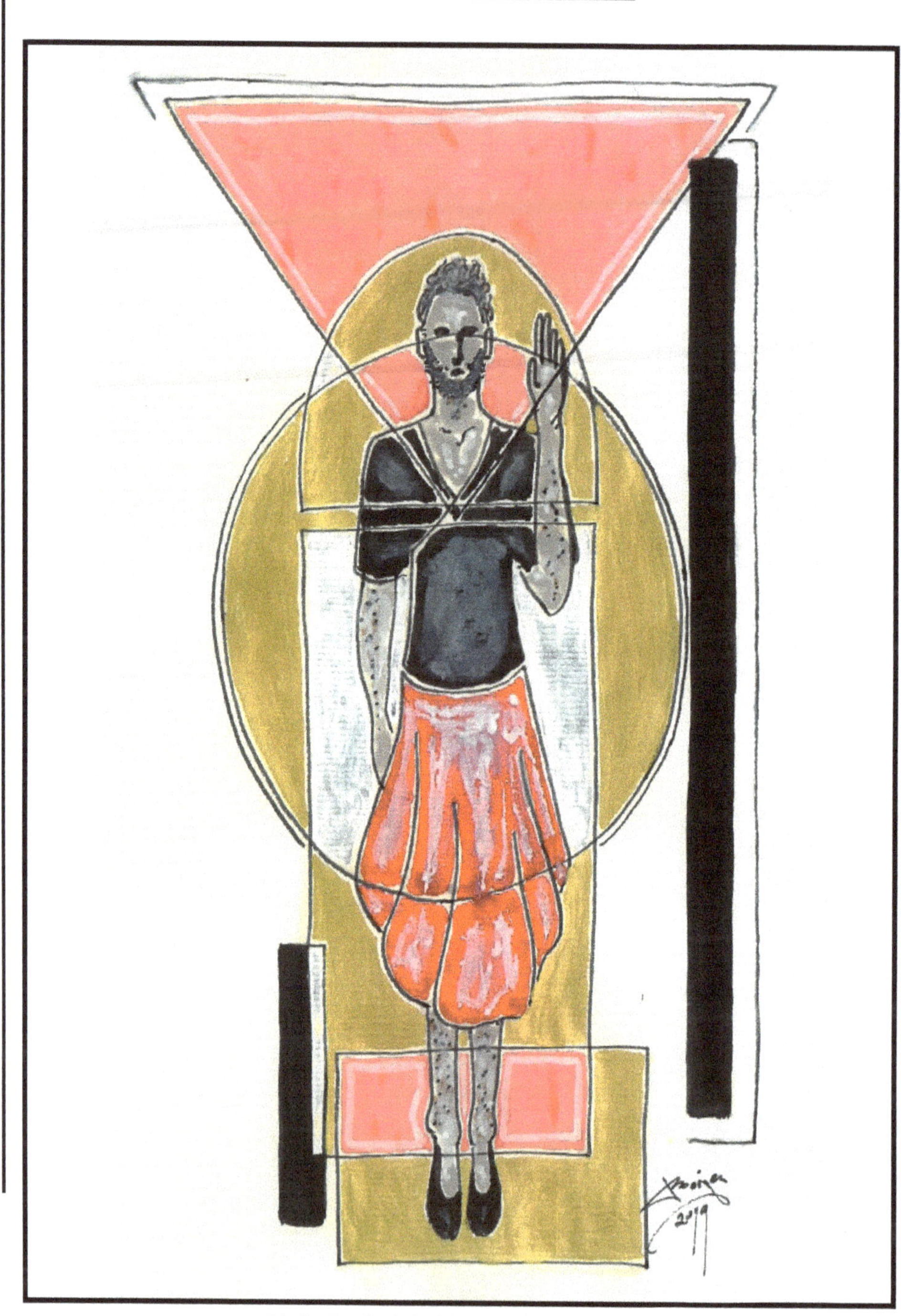

Motherland Died of Cancer, the Citizen Kept on Waving in Vain

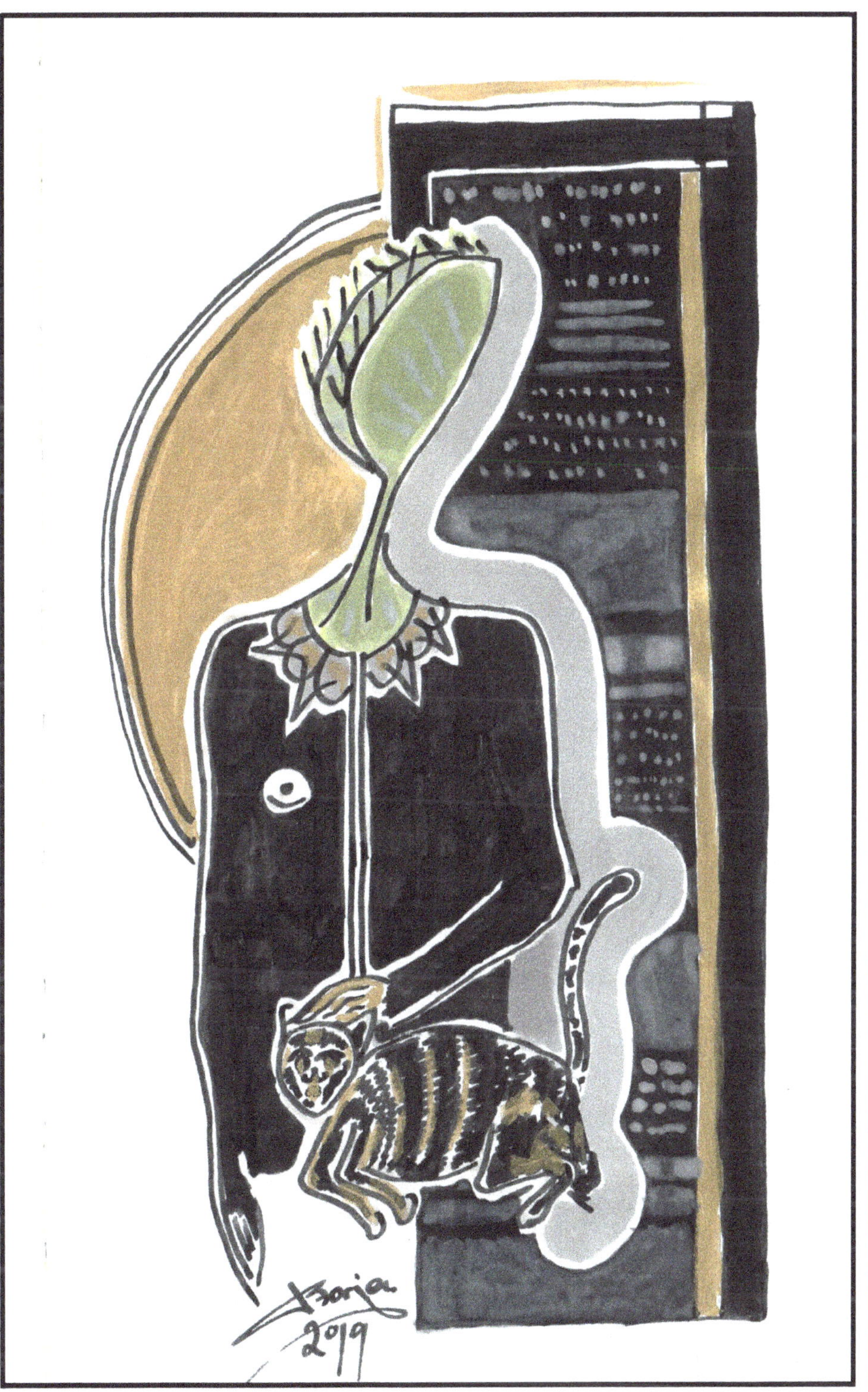

A Carnivorous Relationship Comes with a Gift Cat, or Venus Flytrap, Madonna of the Stripes

# Midwestern nativity

Katherine Lutz

A backdrop—rows of reaching,
leafless oak trees—darkens
the field's edge. Its young grass in
lowness, punctuated by bloomless wildflowers. Sunlight
and breeze graze their surface
like outstretched hands and
circle back to dry,
sporadic clouds.

Light drops
back to the field's center,
where a scarecrow, unnatural,
stands guard. It has no helmet, no weapon.
No eyes or mouth painted on its canvas head. I walk
to its eyeless stare and breastplate
made of withered brass.
The armor's patina weeps
green into the soil.

Hugging its shoeless
feet are sun-kissed, hairy weeds—
airy progeny of the first dandelions, white
and candid. Children of decomposition, nature pushing time
by creating who-ing homilies of soon-
to-be dead things.

Dandelions sprout too yellow—a distinctly different
shade than death. Rewind and
start again.

# Isaac On His Way to the Slaughter

*Bruce J. Berger*

How sharp into my childlike wrists were those leather thongs by which you bound me tightly to that outcropping of rock when I knew you were about to take my life, and how sharp was the edge of that blade when you tested it against your thumb to draw a thin line of blood, and yet much sharper you made it when you honed it against the whetstone you'd hidden under the folds of your robe.

And it was all so clear to me that I would be the victim of your urge to kill, that you'd already killed a fair share of sheep and goats in offerings to your god and that the blood spilled hadn't been enough, it had in fact stirred your thirst for even more. And I saw you drink it, saw you scorn the strict rules you'd always preached to me, rules that your god had supposedly decreed about the taking of life, rules that I once thought you truly believed.

But then I saw you couldn't resist the temptation to become powerful through slaking your thirst with life. My mother saw me staring secretly at your ritual and pulled me away, turned my face toward her as if by doing so she could erase the image, and she bade me never speak of it, but I couldn't forget that look of exquisite delight on your face.

And when you set off with me to find a special place for sacrifice, it had to have been like a stab in my mother's heart, and she knew the pain of losing her only child, knew it was the last she'd see of me, knew that her god punished her for her sin against Hagar and Ismael, and knew she could say nothing, not even goodbye, would do nothing to stop you, and kept her silence.

No place for me to run. The wilderness in its terrible beauty would've devoured me in a day and the buzzards would've picked clean my bones in a night and I would've died alone. Maybe I shouldn't have feared that ending, maybe that would've been better than being blind and deceived, just disappearing from life as I'd appeared slowly from a putrid speck entered into my mother's womb, but I wanted the nearby comfort of a murdering father more than I feared the ripping of your knife, and marched obediently alongside your donkey, measuring my last steps, counting each step, reliving in my mind as much as I could of the short life I'd lived.

So I was ready, and when I asked you "Where is the sacrifice, *Abba*?" it was my paltry effort at sarcasm, because you knew I knew. God would provide indeed. I was ready, I saw no point in resisting.

You heard a voice, you say, calling "Abraham! Abraham!" I would've heard it too, if that's how it had happened, but I heard nothing. I felt the knife touch my throat, and by that time I wanted nothing more than to have it over and done with. Just that light touch drew its own thin line of blood, and I couldn't understand why you didn't send me to sleep with our ancestors at once. I couldn't understand why the cut was not sharp and deep and immediately deadly, as you'd have done a sheep or goat, why you had not let all my blood gush out in a bright red stream until my heart had pumped my entire being onto the grey rocks and the barren earth around us.

Then I felt the touch of your finger on my throat, coating itself with blood from that thin and shallow crevasse in my neck, and then I heard you lick that finger and smack your lips, and I knew that the ordeal was over.

You'd had your wish, and the superficial wound in my neck would heal with time, and the slight scar would be visible beneath my beard only to Rebekah, who never believed this story.

# Preparing the Body for Resurrection

*Andrew Hutto*

**A Memo to Employees of SACRED BURIAL®**
**Protection Against Rot, and Expertise in Religious Preservation**

You must do the following as the Lord our God has commanded:

Tie a red ribbon around His wrist,
           put snow in His ears.
Cover His mouth in vermillion lace.
Put a hubcap under His head so that He may rest.
Spray Drakkar Noir™ in between the toes.

     Wrap His cock in tin foil.
     Lay peonies across the collar bones.

Insert pebbles from the Sea of Galilee into the hole in His side.

Give Him a bandolier made of Christmas lights,
           (there should be an outlet to the left of the bear's den,
           in the back of the cave.)
Position His right hand in salute.

Drape His chambers in party streamers and Charmeuse silk.

Put a subway token on the left eye, and a buffalo nickel on the right.

     Roll a red carpet from tombstone to Emmaus

Resist the urge to take flash photographs for this may cause
unnecessary degradation of the body which
we so solemnly want to preserve.

Lastly, before I thank you for your swift and urgent work,
remember to leave the crown of thorns untouched.

# What even are Thou?

Jeff Scott Lane

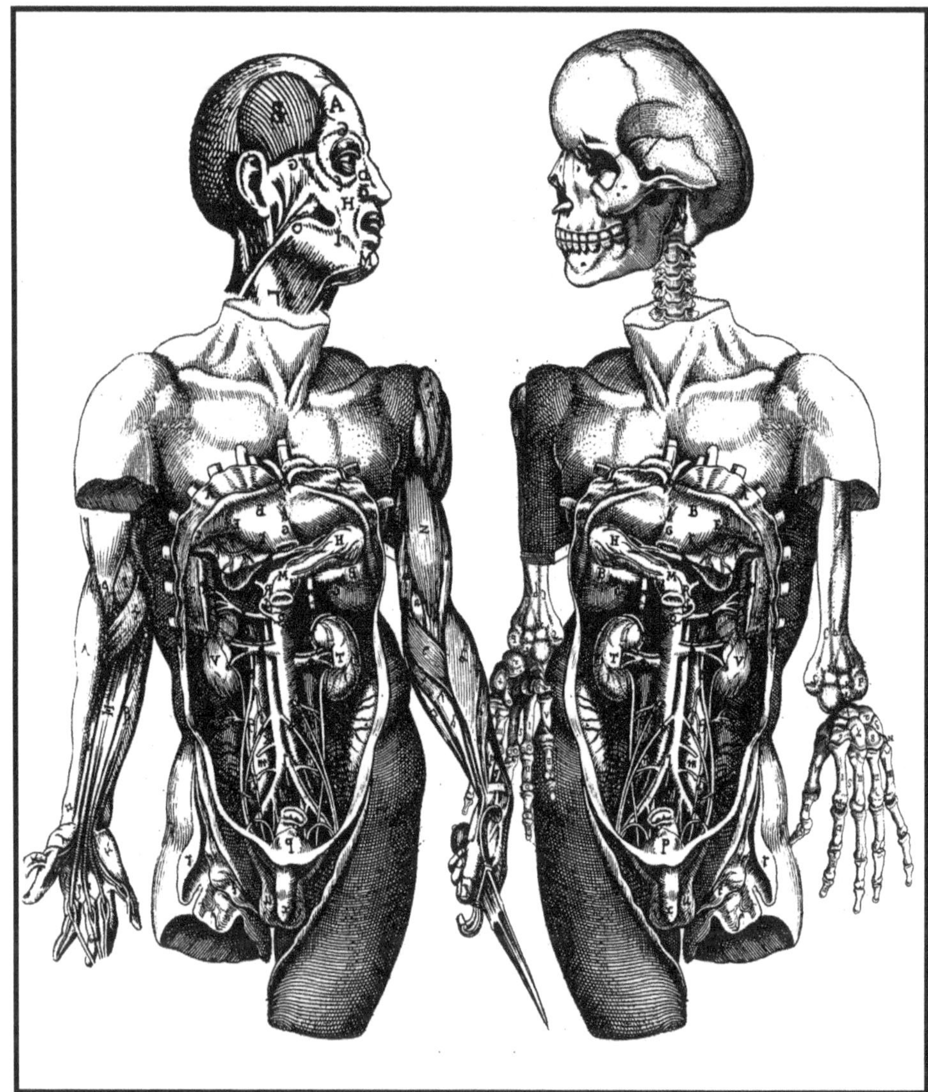

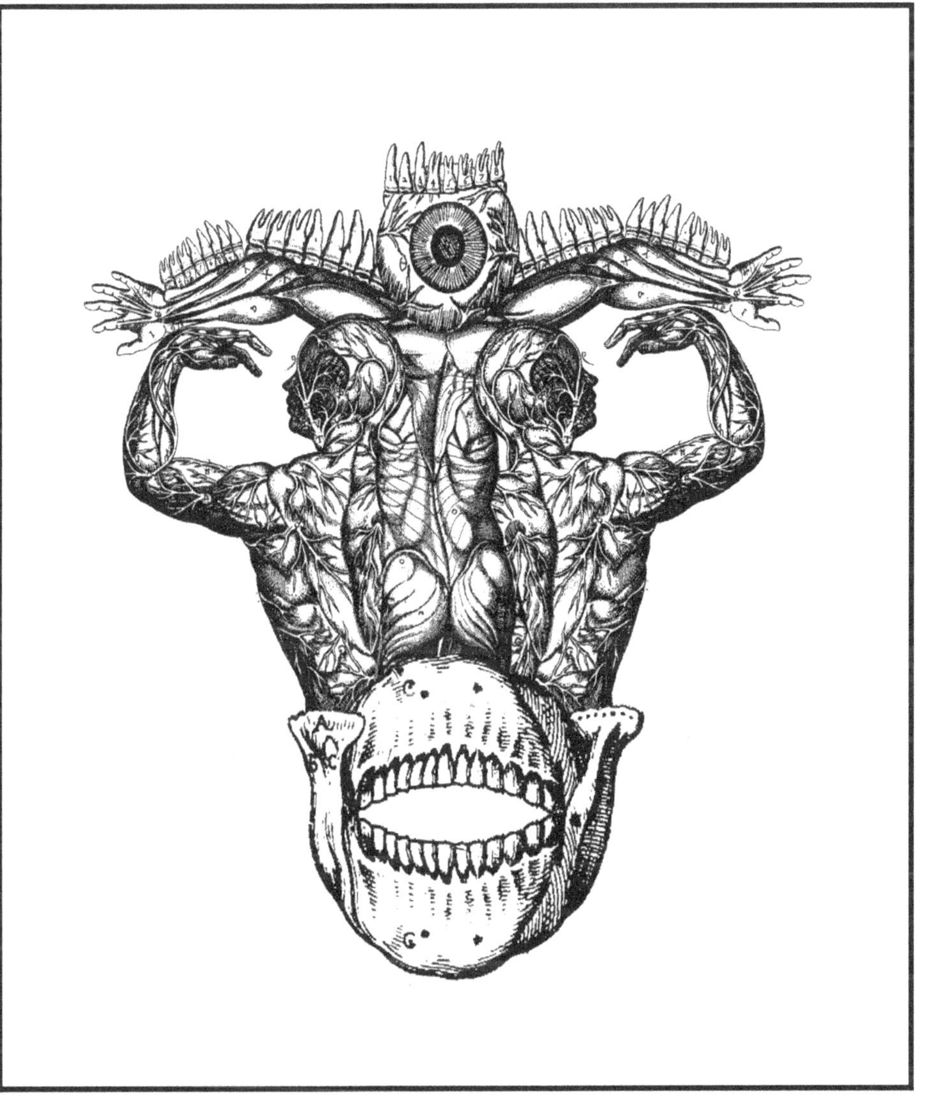

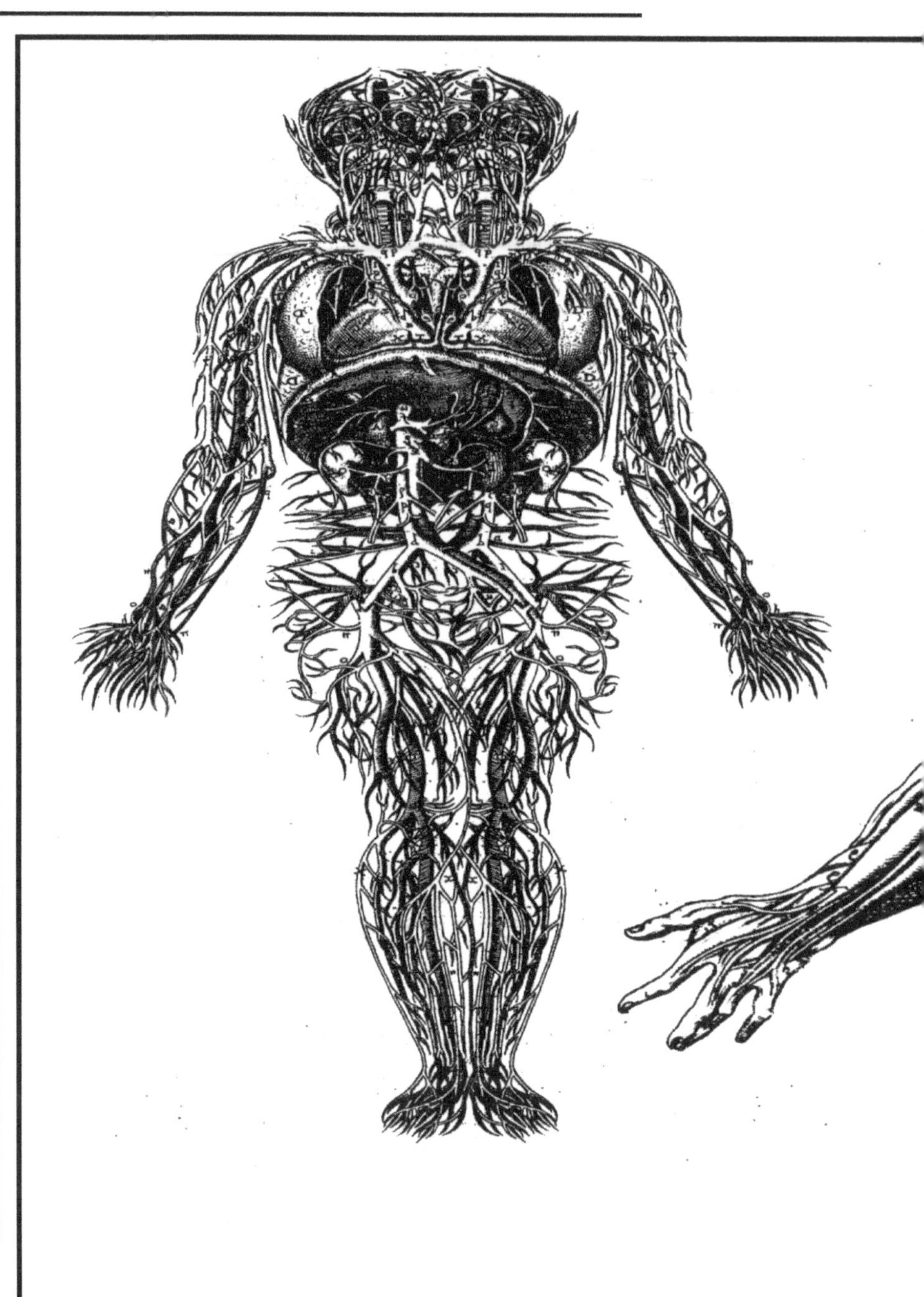

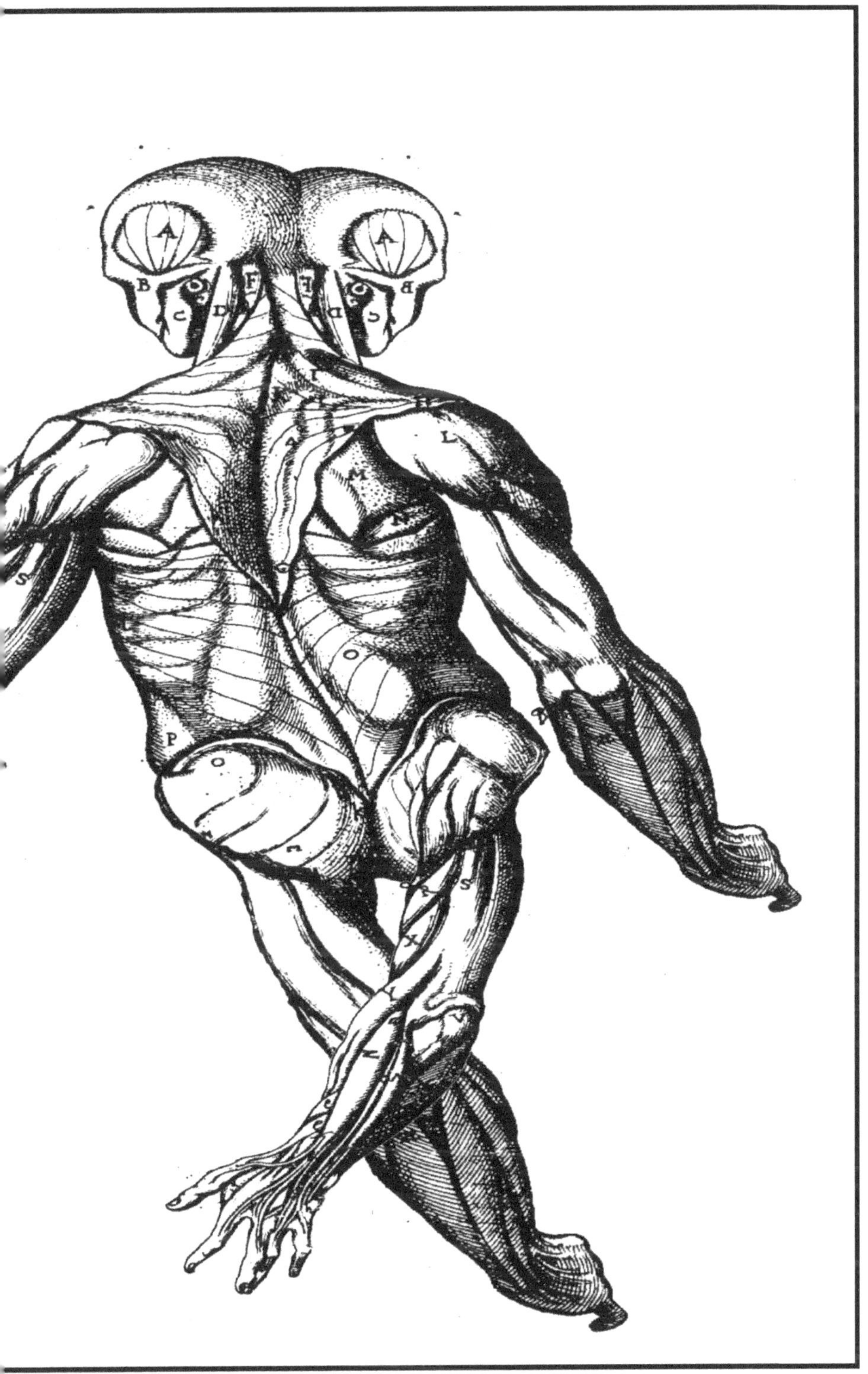

A
A
B
C
D
F
F
D
C
B
I
L
L
M
N
G
O
P
O
R
Q
G
R
S
X
V
S

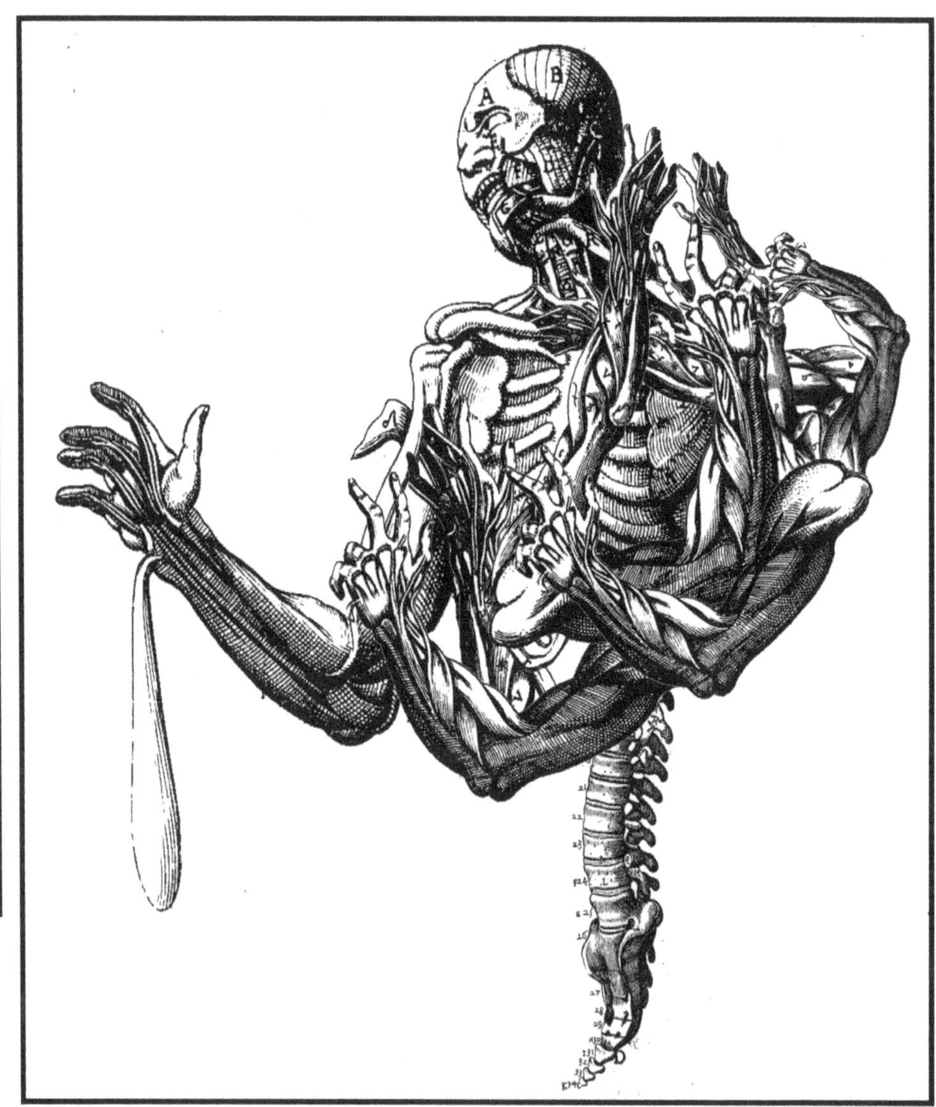

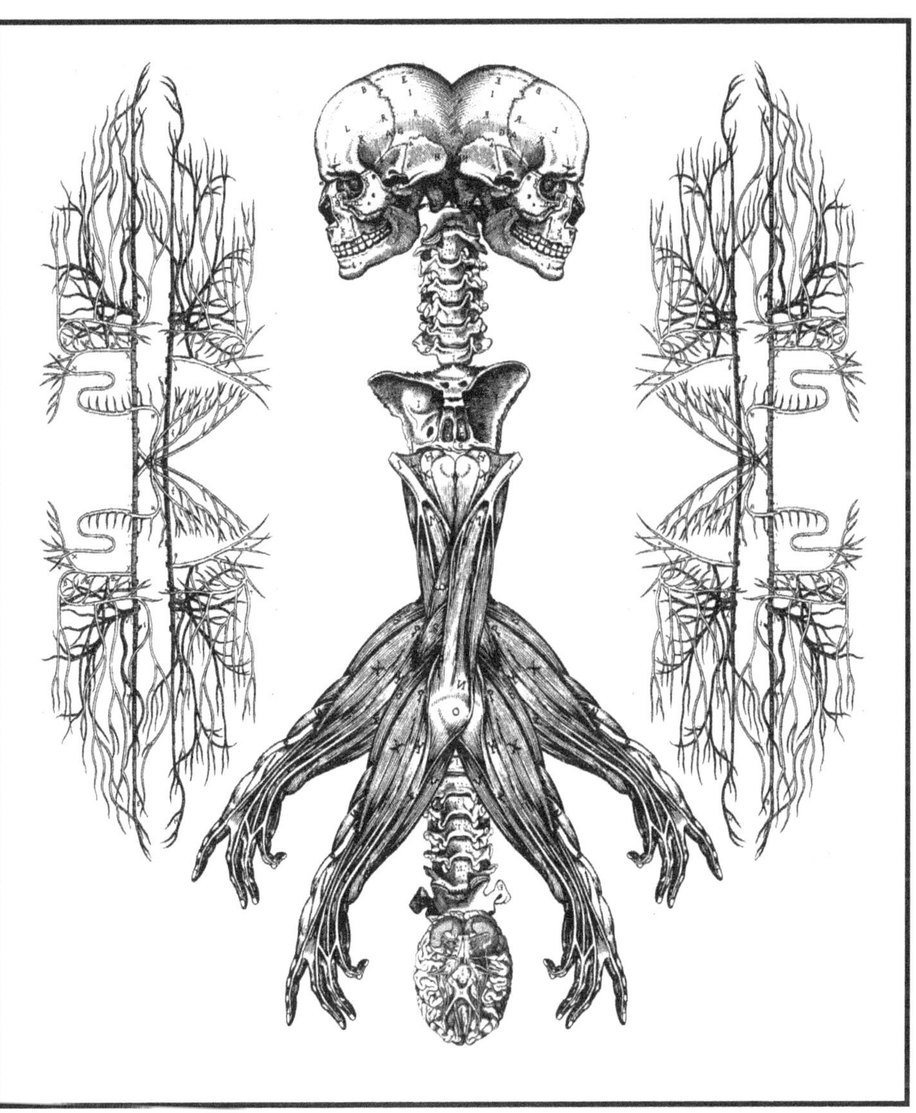

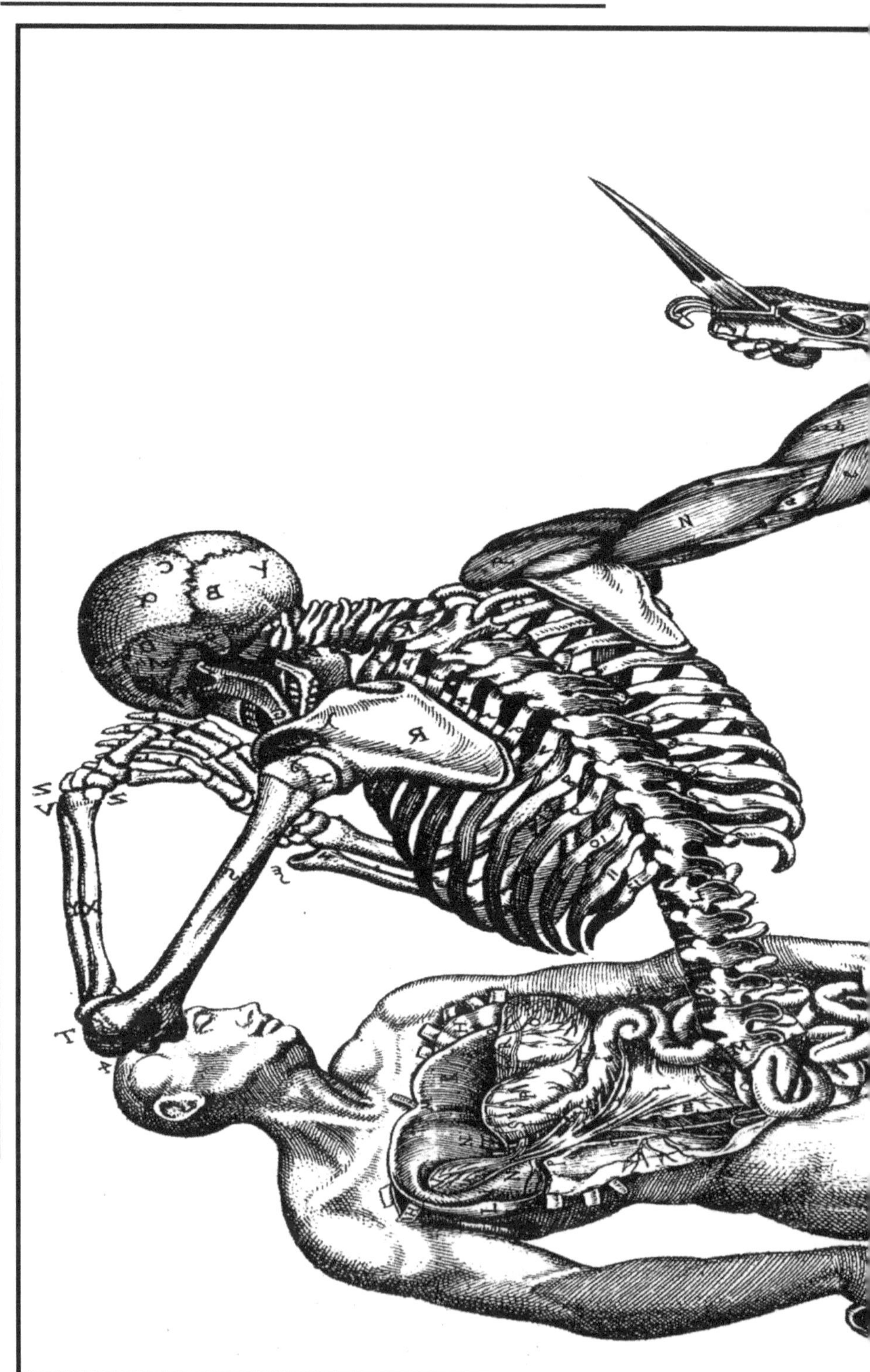

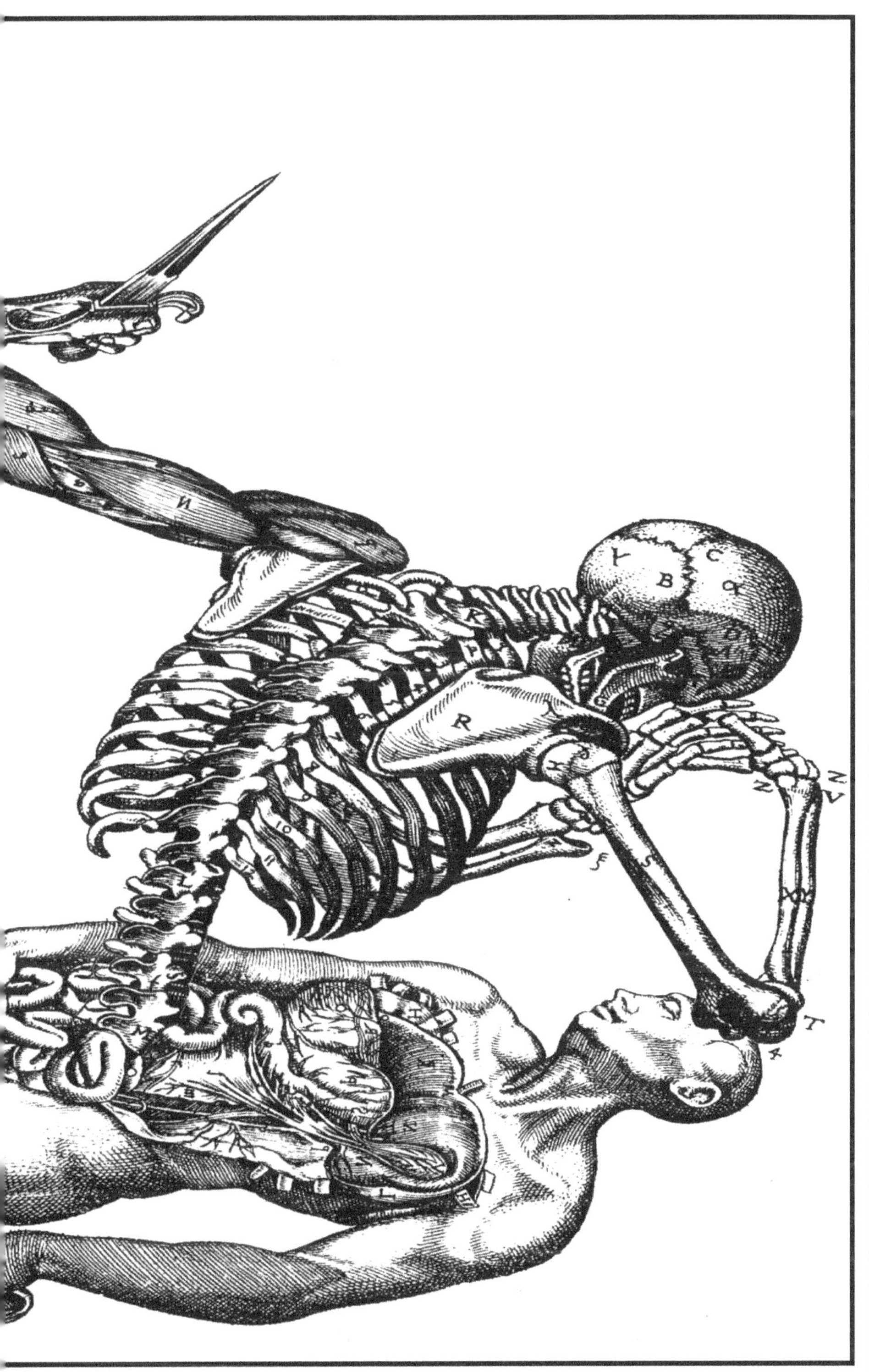

# Waiting Room

Tim Stiles

Thin gray sweater.
Fuzzy white socks.
Trifocals. Toothbrush. Colgate.
Still-good 1978 Avon hair brush.
Her favorite Harriet Beecher Stowe.

All that—
Ma's life in a plastic sack.
He holds it tight while we wait,
My father's million-dollar bag.

# Your Garden and the Praying Mantis

*Sara Dallmayr*

*For Rick*


The abdomen of an adult mantis

Is covered with wings. One scalding


Afternoon you dripped under a black

Shirt and told me how a mantis nods


Its wings in flight at you, in the air

A hint of green, rusted blades.


The moon tilts, a succession of

Saucers aloft in an expanse of blue.


Dark overgrown summer, thick

With undertow, rooms so deep


Iridescent fathoms which brood

Before a storm, bow to the thunder


Heads, an engine throttle. In the arch

Over the tulips where the fireworks


Grew restless and flew into the garage,

As if we were a rogue target. Such are


The days unwinding anymore, we forget

How to plan, and unfold our shirts that is

If we remembered to fold them while they
Were still warm. The paramedics took hours.

You took time off the wall and played
With its hands, shook its face. Time said

Nothing. The scaffold and the cautious
Creeping gnomes, a swarm of daffodils

Scrape the side of the garage. You spoke
Of your own death long ago, unafraid

In the room with ripples on the ceiling,
An echo of aging paint and restless wings.

# WYETH AND METROPOLITAN

*Leon Fedolfi*

A nomination of Blackbirds -
Each wing beats a second of creation
As Seven Universes
Pass lazily through a summer day -

A slip of lemonade.

A Quintillion Blackbirds sing -
Their songs gather and poise upon dreams for the unborn as
They wait forever.

# Jaipur Roads

Christy Wise

Dust swirled around his legs, trunk, eyes,
not dust from the desert, but dust churned up
by truck tires, horse carts, camel hooves,
tuck-tuck wheels, bicycles, people's feet.

His pace did not vary. Others watched out
for him. Today's load was light: one man
with bundles of textiles, headed to market.

He closed his eyes at the traffic light,
shielding them from insidious dust,
heat, glare, and from flies that swarmed
around his face when he stopped moving.

Parched skin, tired bones ached
for the river, longed to feel coolness
whirling around his haunches, spray
cascading over his dusty back.

But this was Monday morning,
in the heart of Jaipur, with a full
week ahead. Not that the elephant
counts days or even knows
what they are.

Yet, he senses that the river is far away

# A Nature, In Place
*Aaron Lelito*

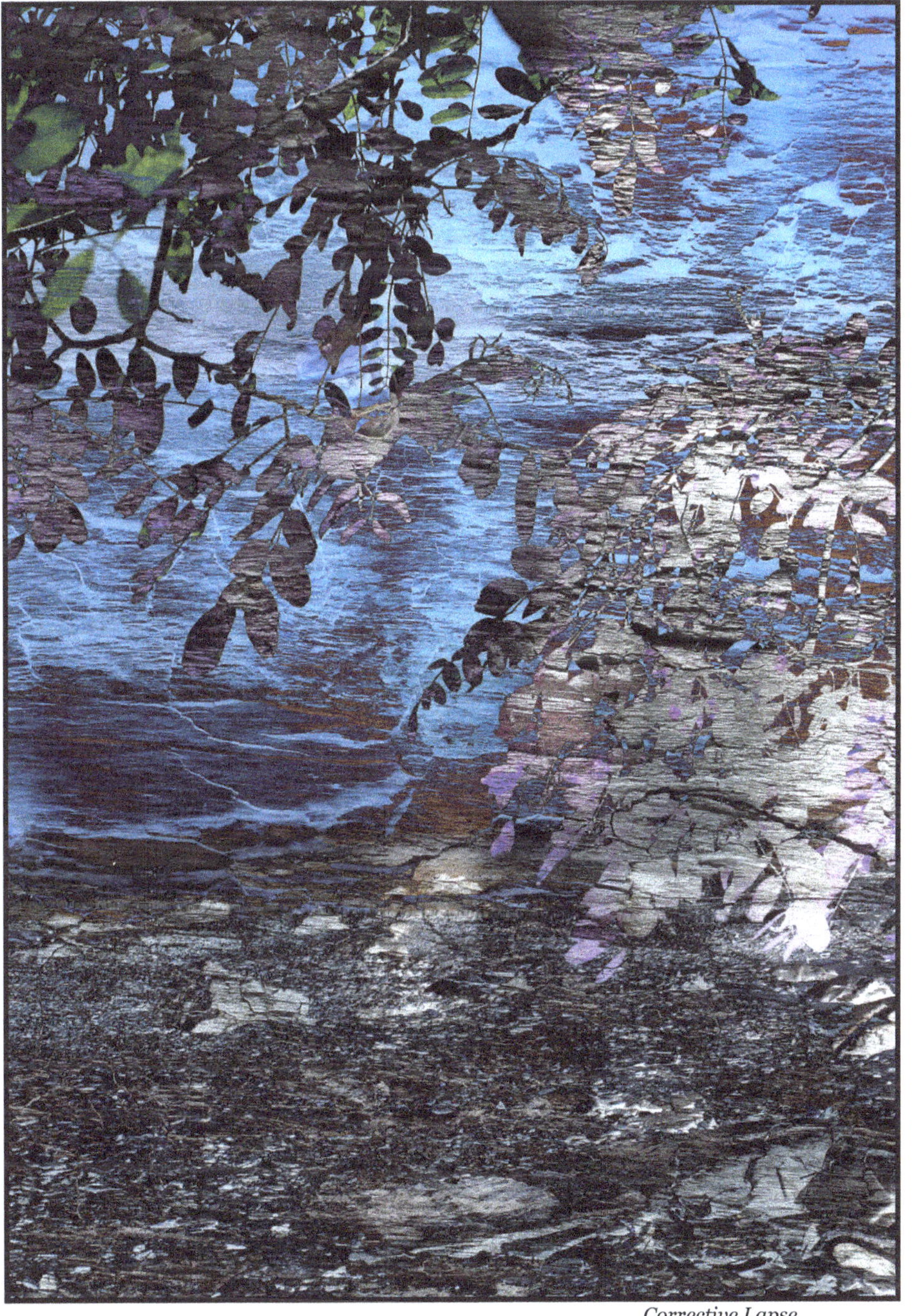

*Corrective Lapse*

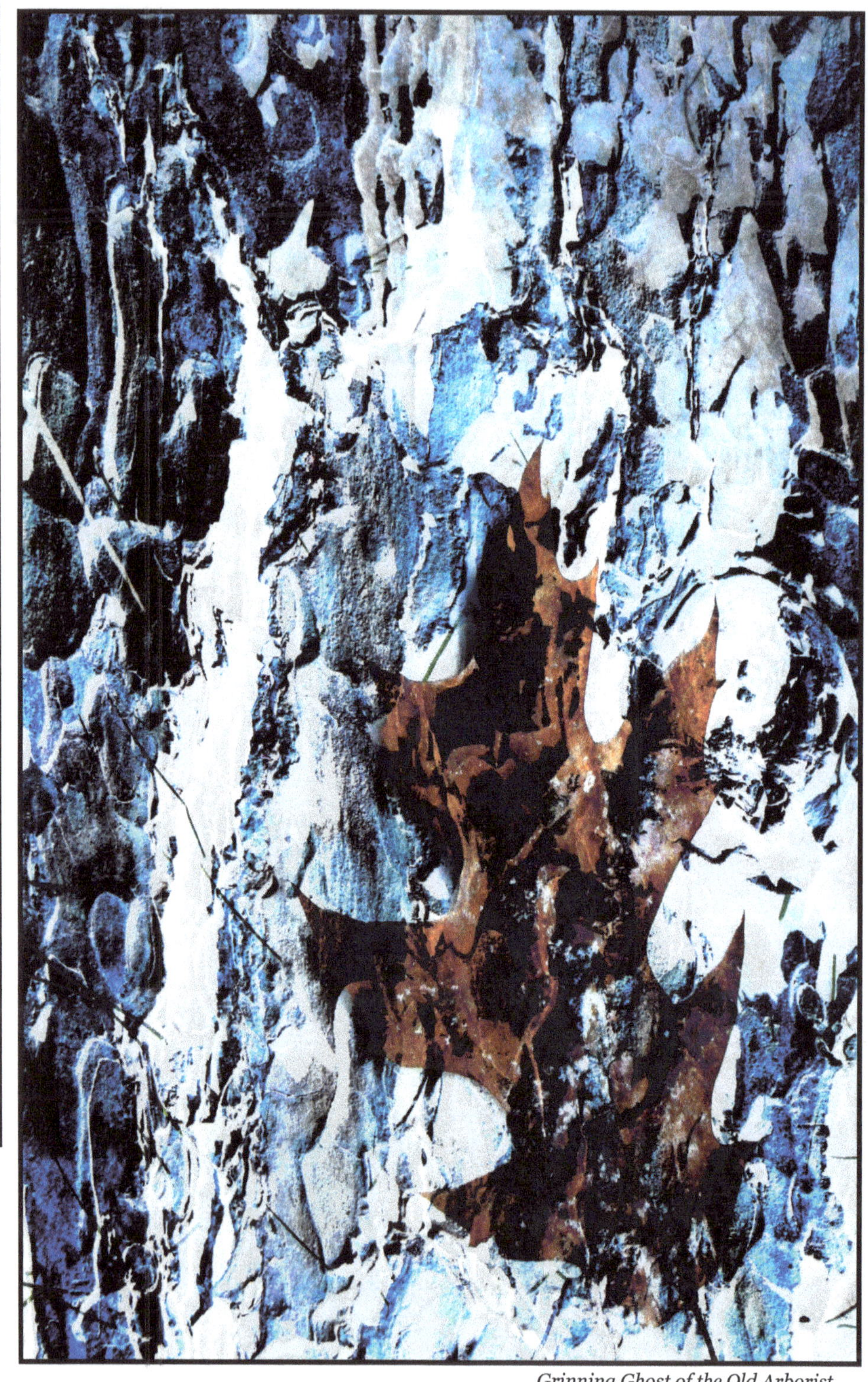

*Grinning Ghost of the Old Arborist*

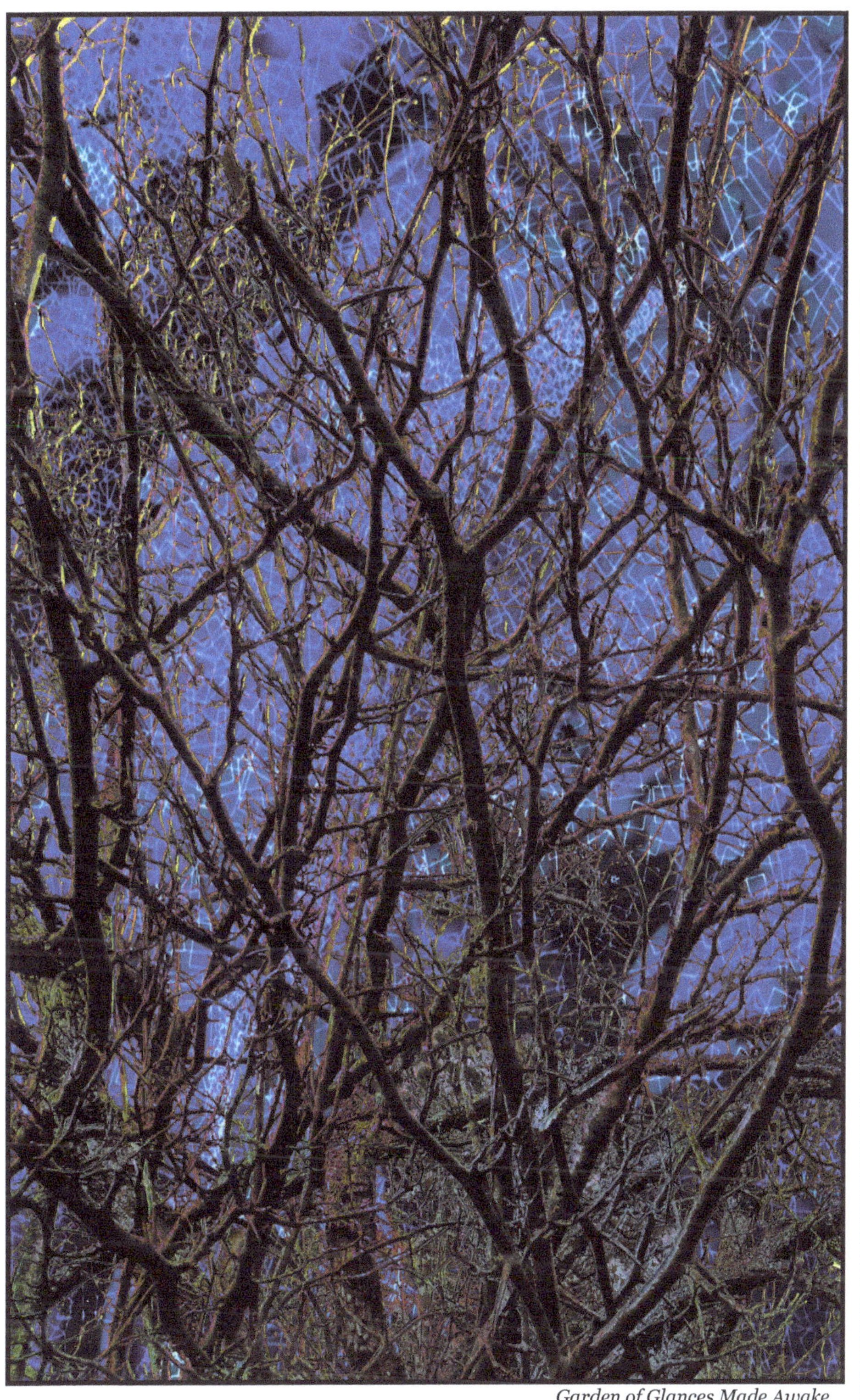

*Garden of Glances Made Awake*

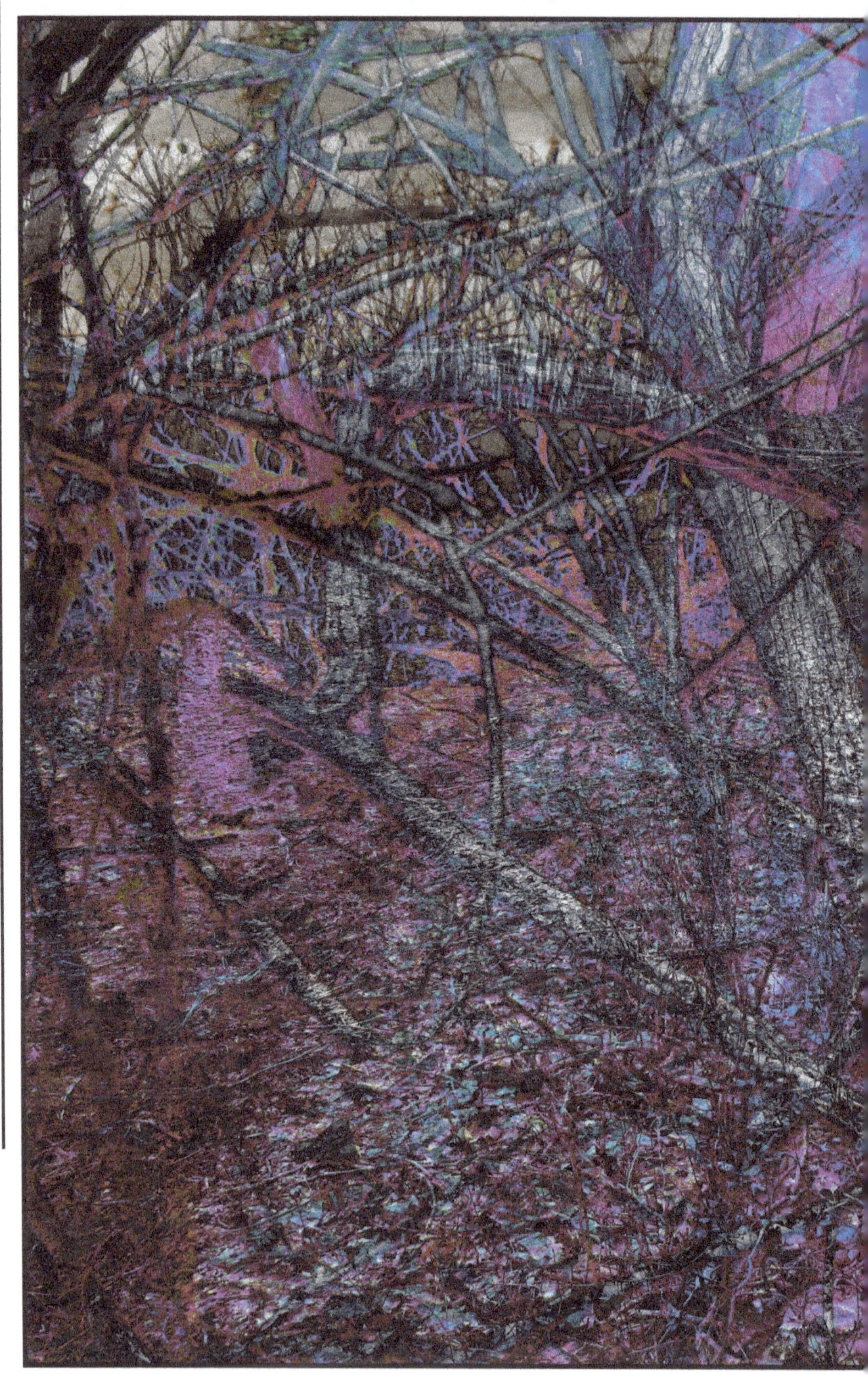

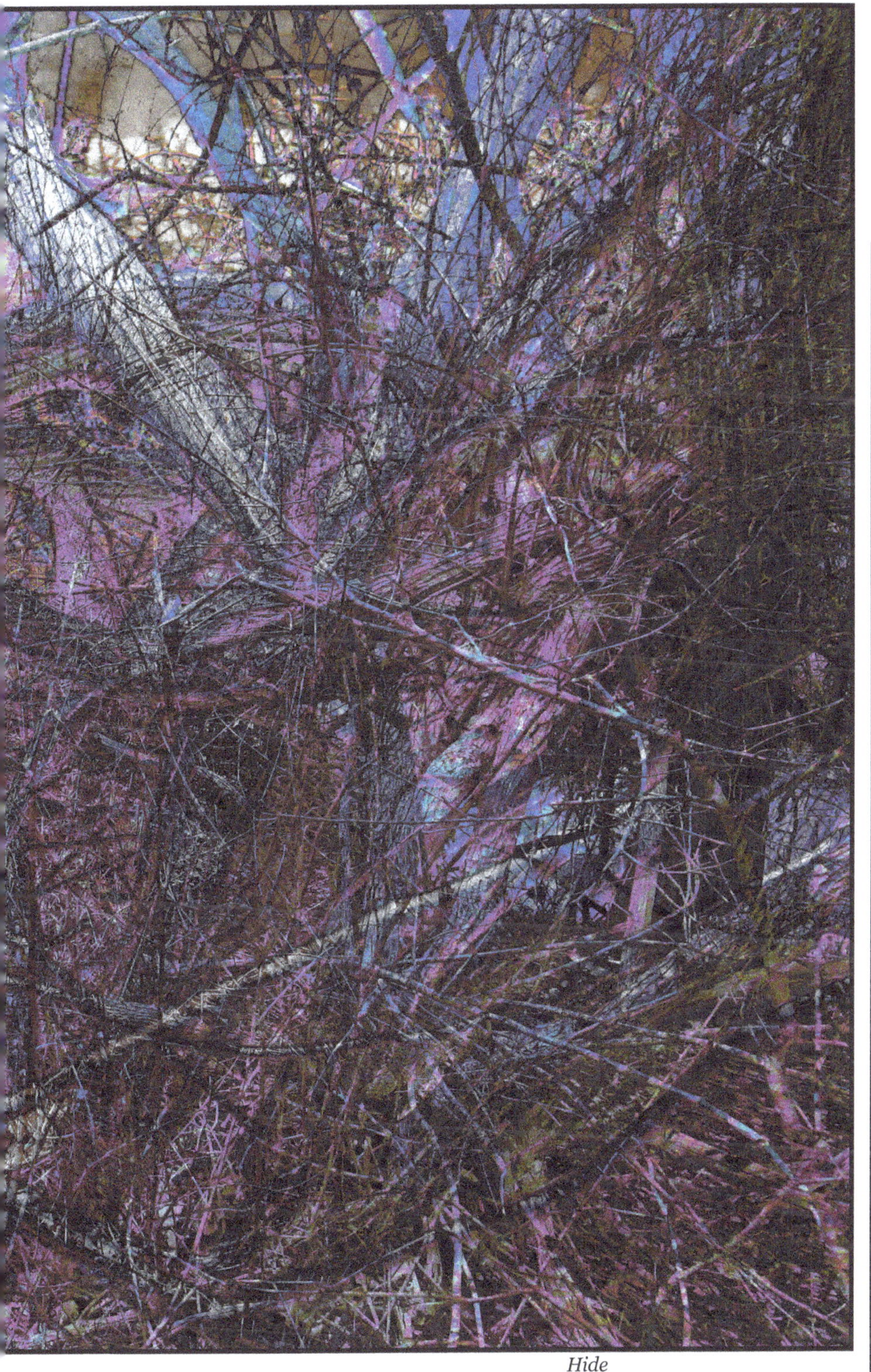

*Hide*

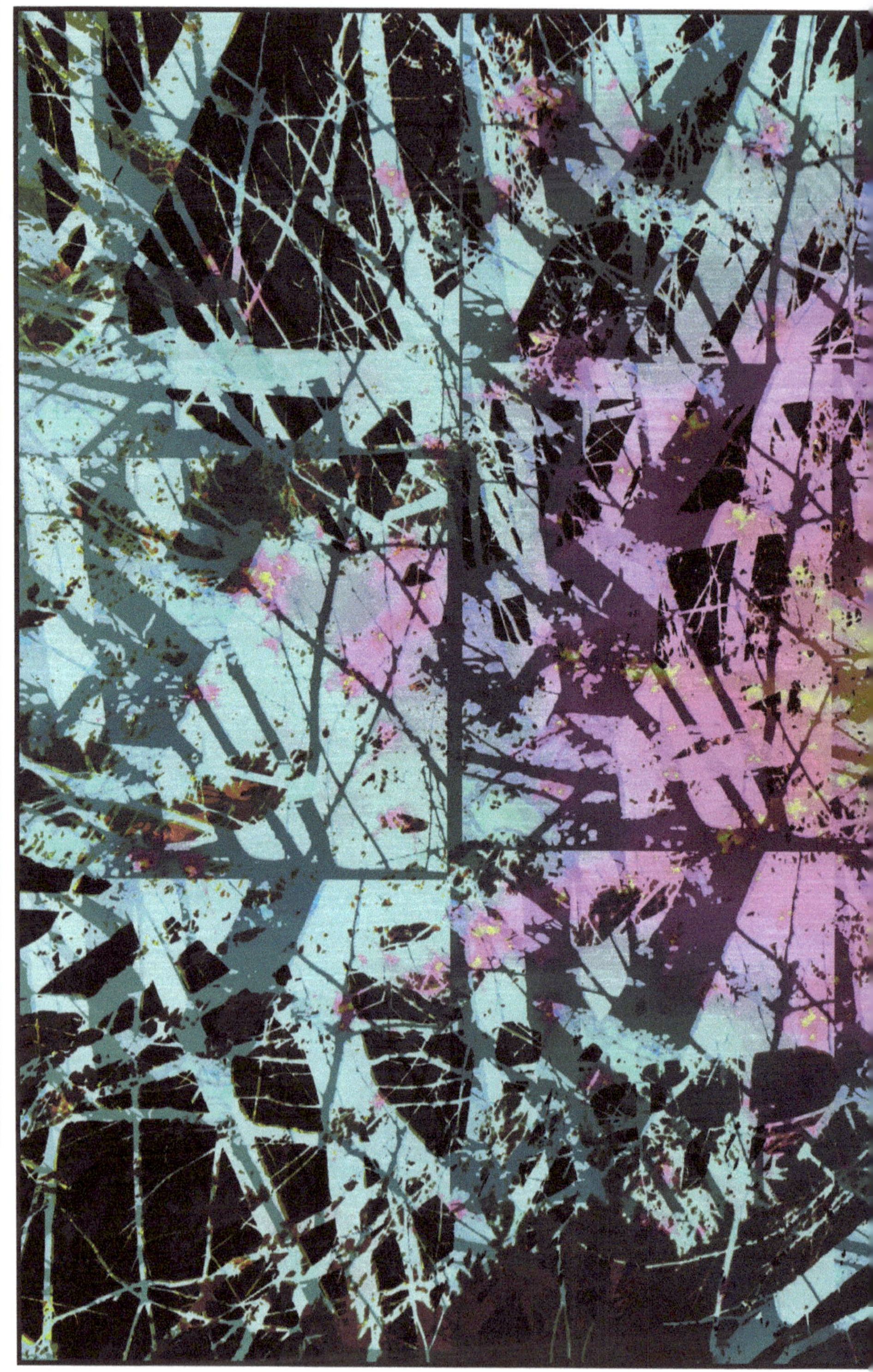

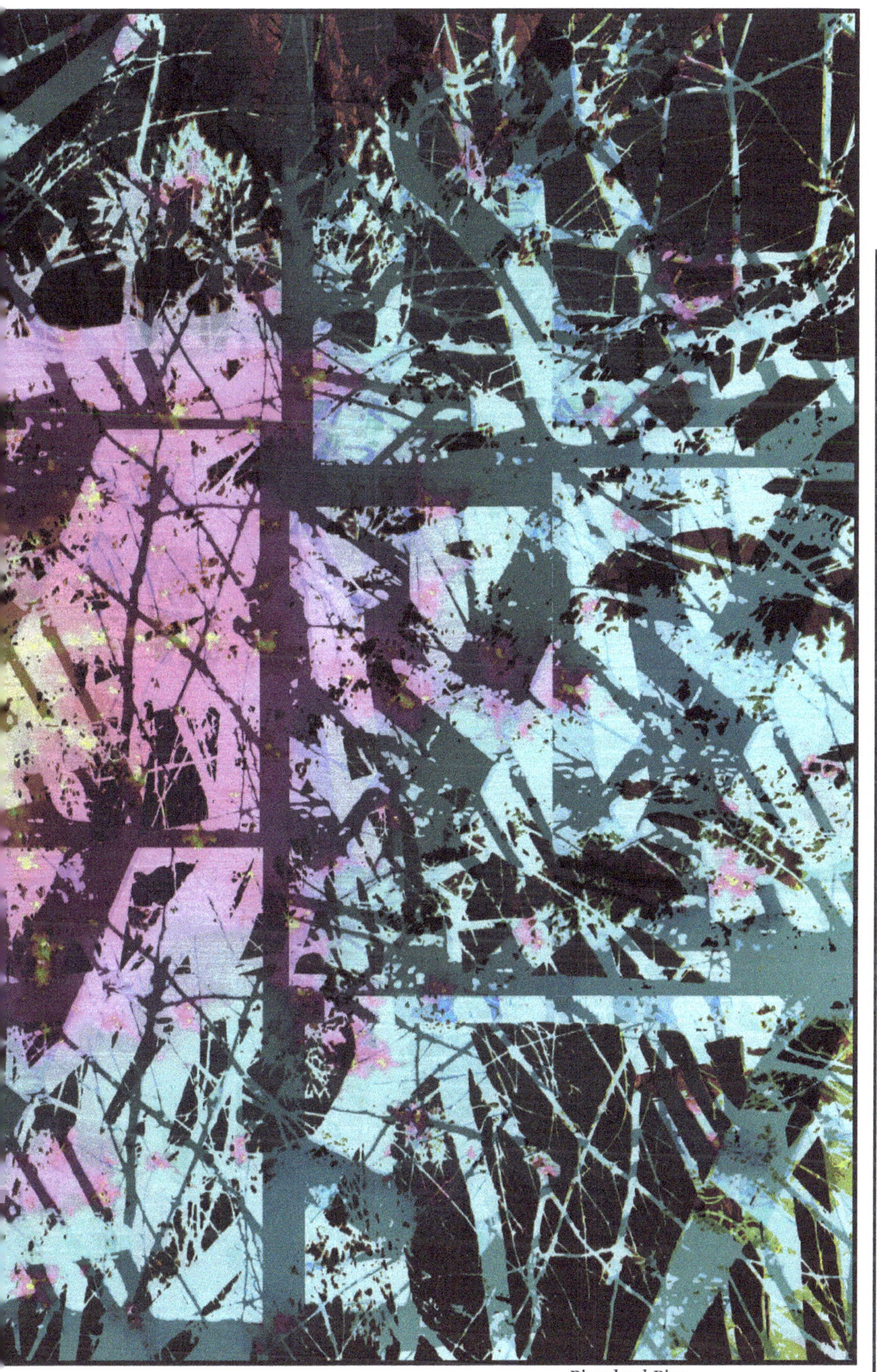

*Pinwheel Pine*

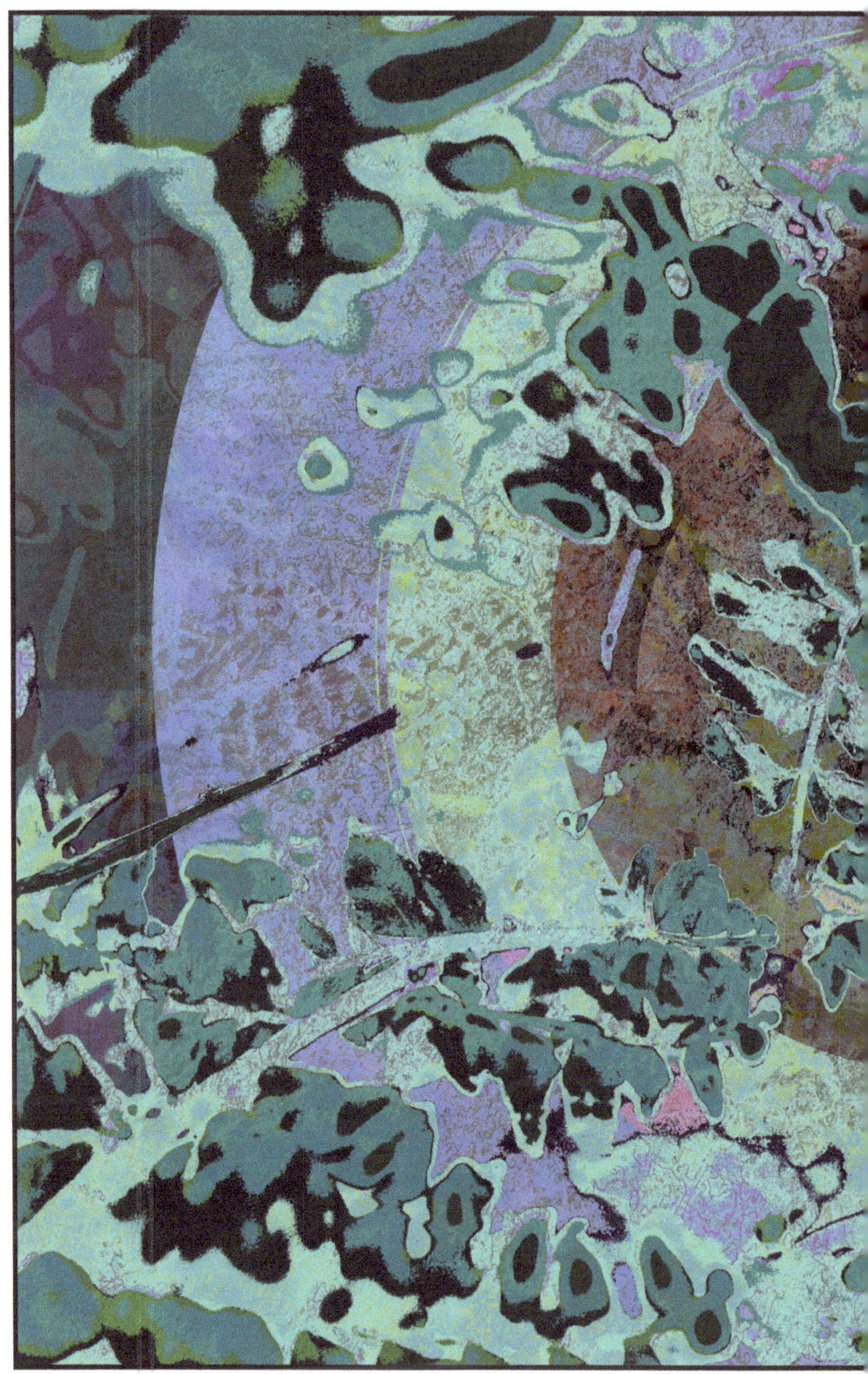

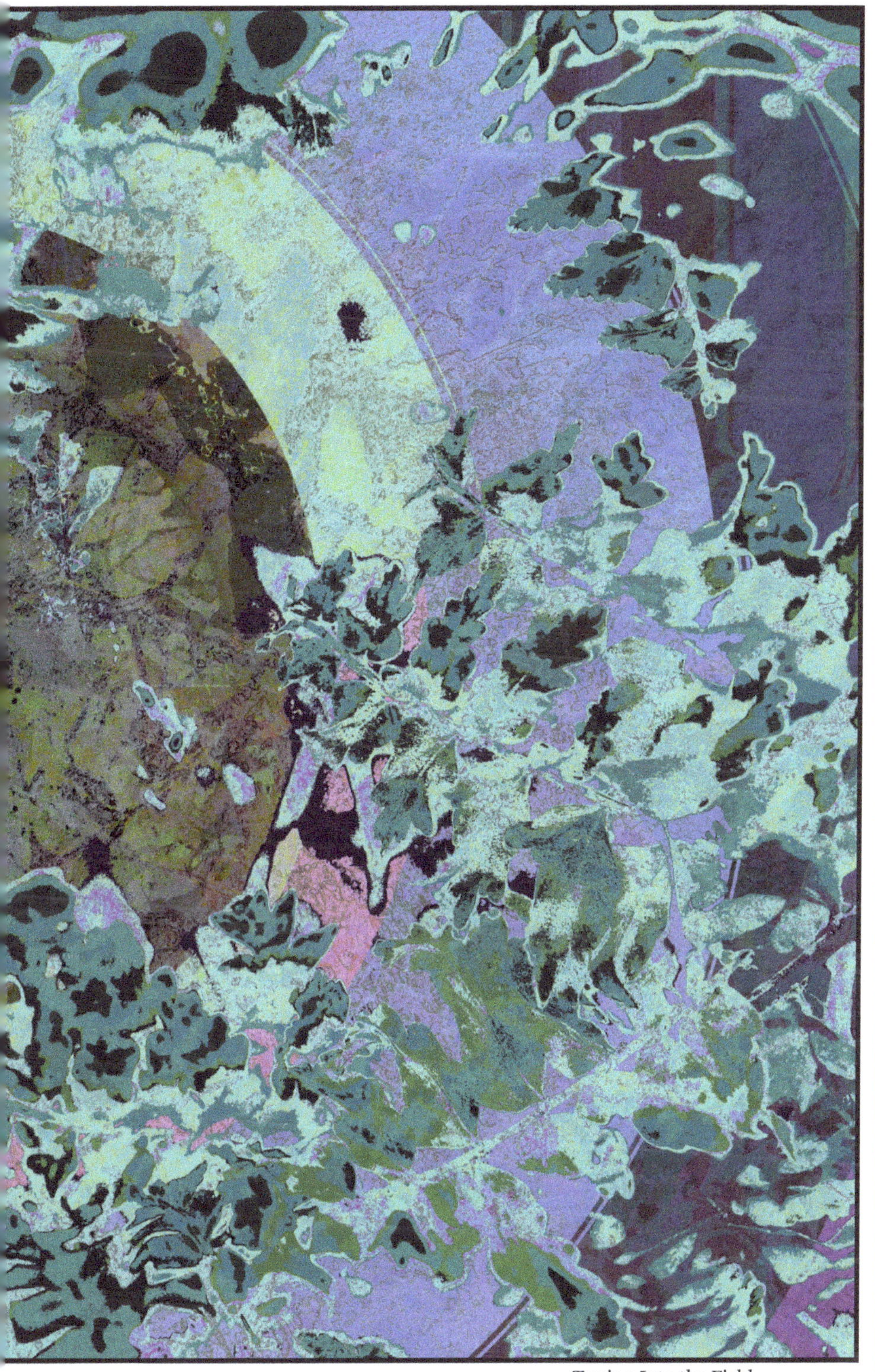

*Tuning Into the Field*

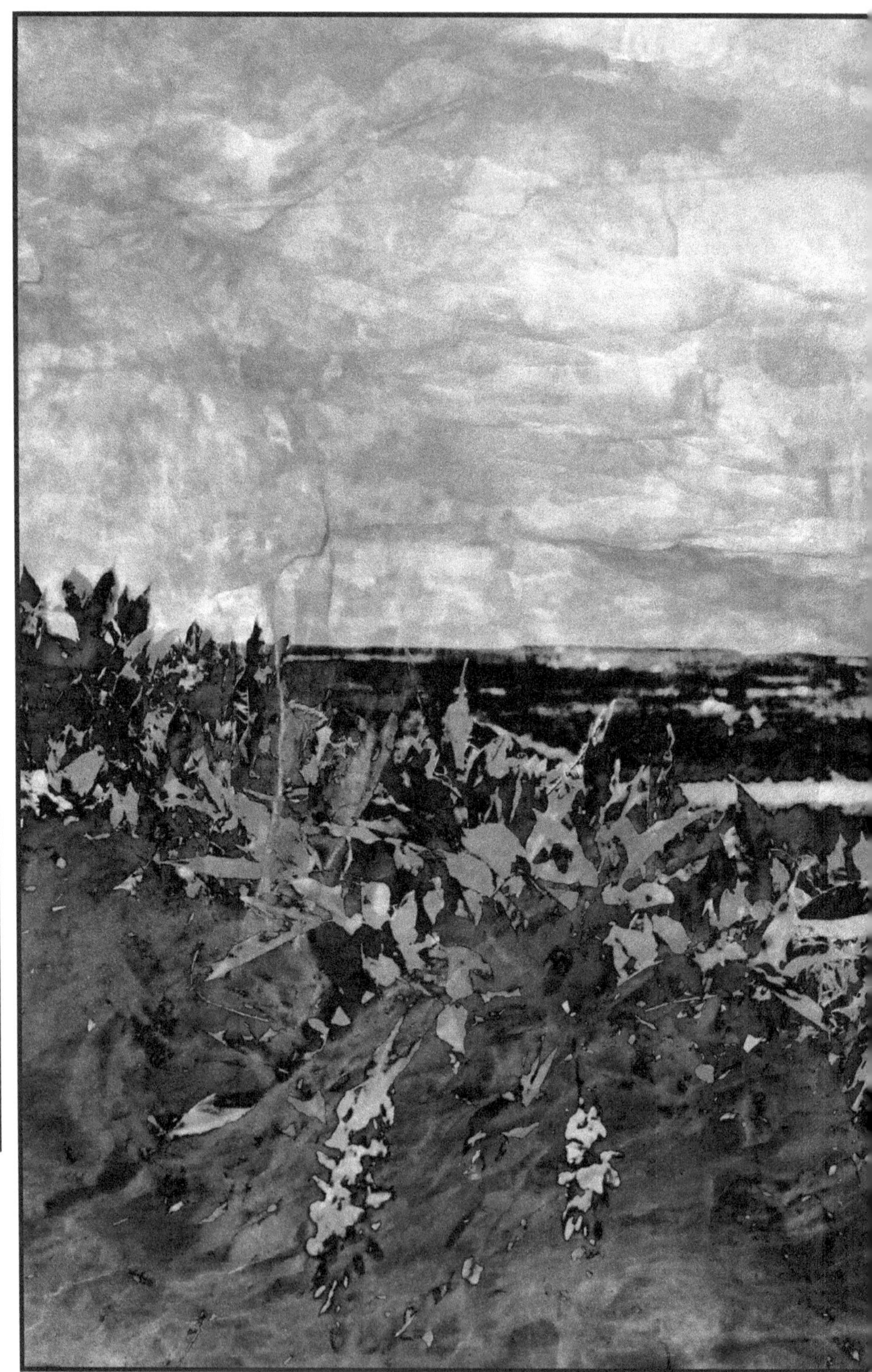

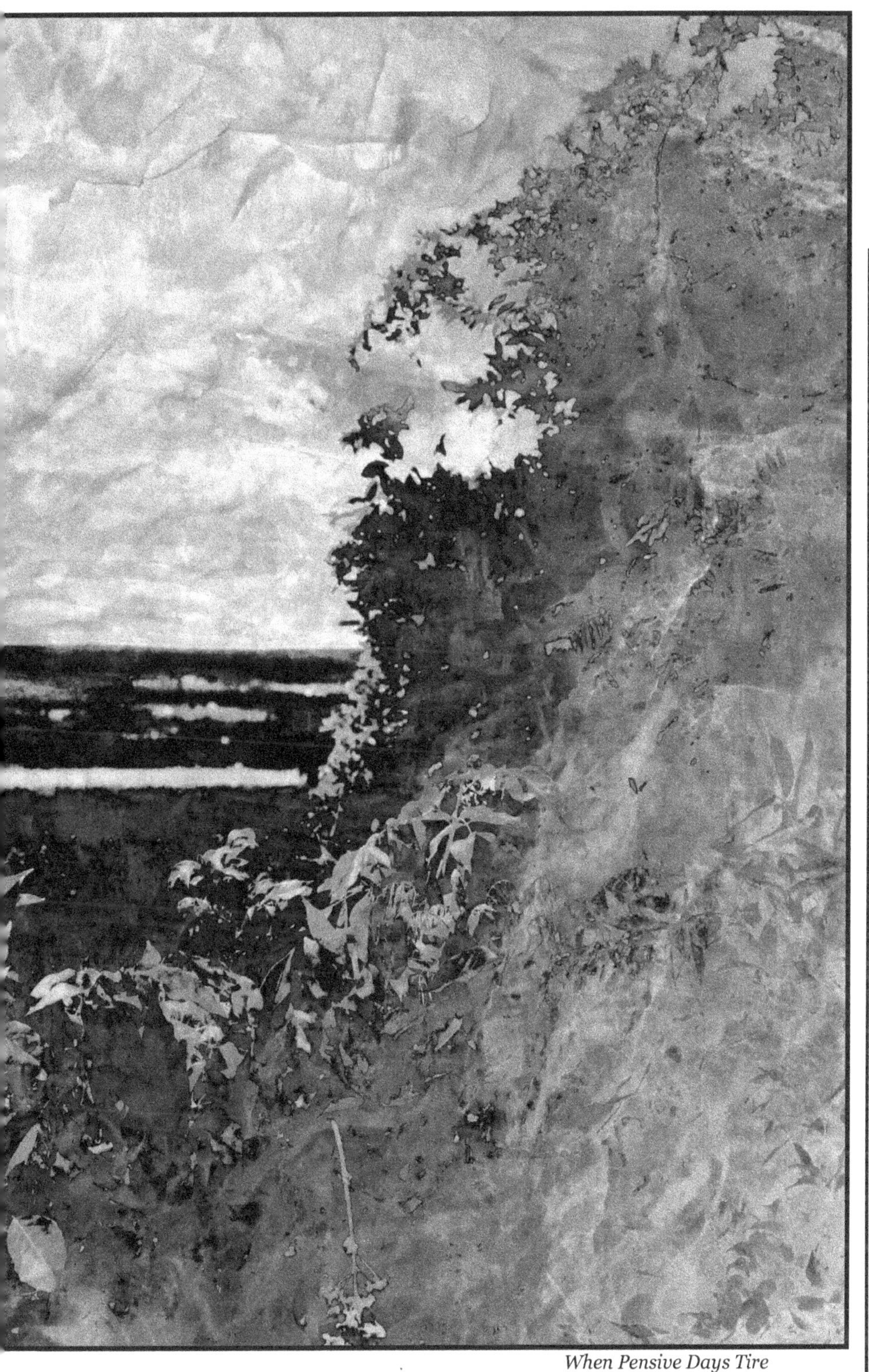

When Pensive Days Tire

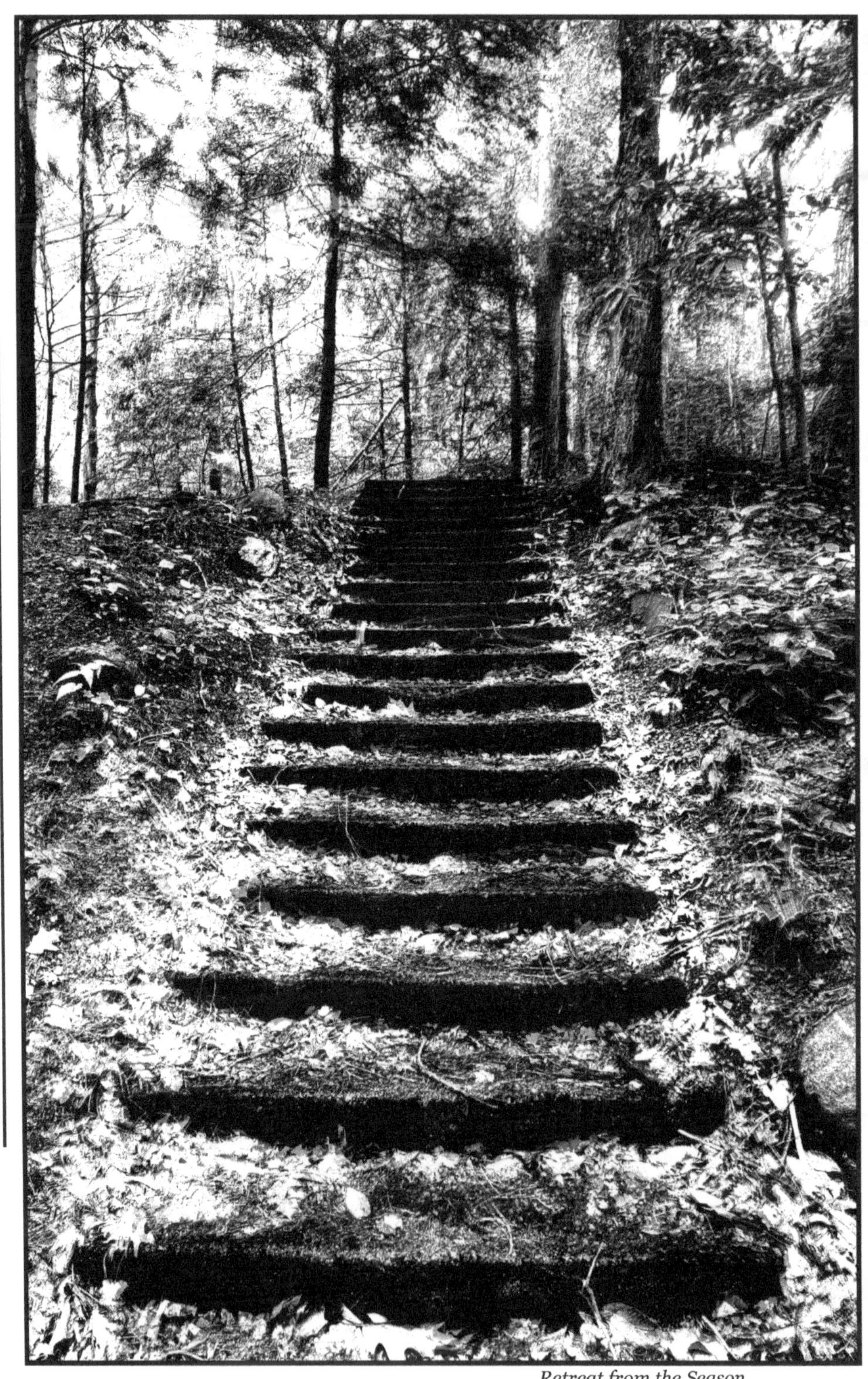

*Retreat from the Season*

# American Corduroy

*Corbin Wamble*

I remember nights of Imessage insults driven through sprinkled streets,
    two white trash wanna be's dueling with roman candles,
carbon dioxide limping off recycled apologies,
    snaking from the muffler to the window of loves
infallible four door sedan, its crash tested, top safety rating.
    Close the garage it's time
to get to business.    Darling
    if I told you I longed for a nightmare, would you believe me?
speaking like a broad who gets off on being tied up
                  spit on

there's a kink between the window and the muffler keeping us alive,
    it's the thrill of suffocation, that ever so incandescent phrase landed
on panting lips, 'choke me' revolving like an elegy to innocence; the animalistic intent
    can't stop won't stop
thrill of looming death, fingering pink piano keys in a dire spring,
    that blonde matinee of american corduroy, clasping starlight and butterflies,
trudging through heavy air, fascinated with the way each stuck to her skin, butterscotch scars
    sprouting honeysuckles; we would have been beautiful if it wasn't for

            God and
        the IRS.

There's news,

    the old hound you loved is dead.
Milky eyed and mean muggin gray, she blindly wandered the house,
    sack bunting loose shoes and goring table legs,
her trash compacted face wrought into that extraterrestrial pecan swirl.
    A seizure took her while I worked, she died alone in the living room
looking like a botched acid trip, her spellbound smirk half relieved,

half terrified, the scent of unbrushed fangs cloaked in expelled bowls,
hoisted to heaven in a black leather La-Z-Boy.
      I imagine this to be the pinnacle of modern death, hairy pride and


                                      the diarrheal

                             ascension.

Do you remember
      the night we went dancing?
your dress too tight to drop it low, my pride
      too high to admit you were taller than me in heels,
 you tugged at coattails as if the
      existential wind were inching up your skirt,
trying to cop a feel with a newly cracked Pabst


                       gripped like a rose.


When we leapt off the porch to go to the shore,
      I gave you that hackneyed promise
I'm still convinced is worth something only once,
      that first time I expelled it out of instinct        starved wolf pack depravity
like a promise to God in a moment of terror, you can't shut it out,
      can't mute your own repression, can't cannibalize your own words


                                 not anymore;


You returned it on the zenith of the bridge, steel tongue grafted over the inlet,
      the charter vessels roaring in sync with boiling passion


                           You spoke reluctantly,


as if choking on something you'd been meaning to say
      but never could

still to this day
          never could;

                                        held over my head,

some

             meant-to-be-broken-take-twice-a-day-with-food-promise.

I went on huffing salt as if trying to wake from a dream,
          staring over the sapphire expanse of the Atlantic,
wondering how such darkness could mirror the stars.
In the gravel lot years before we parted, the sky was a snapdragon,
          citrus clouds seemed to stare with fiery eyes,
 I knew it was just God watching me make mistakes,
          cloaking wisdom with peregrine wings.
You always hit your head on the roof of the car,
          there was a trampoline rhythm to it,
the sound became our heartbeat, alive and drowned in darkness,
          neon lights leaking from the dashboard,
filling your eyes with psychedelic splendor.
          I stroked your feline back, wrenched over and
dazed in pure love politeness, under spell in shoulders boney grip,
          you levitated in the wake of disaster
like a cherub in the eye of a hurricane,
          voice echoing convictions in a tired rasp.

At christmas,
          my signature naughty-coal-in-stocking-maneuver,
we'd already bought presents so we exchanged
          in a neutral parking lot armistice,
awkward tears brandished
          brash hugs like credit card payments
or post-holiday-poor-gift-returns.

We retreated to separate bunkers
each confided to their own secrets
        folded neatly into wrapping paper cranes.


Those promises were solar flares bleeding off
        tight lipped best-left-forgottens,
like that old hound and her milky eyes
        silently promising me she'd live forever
while we watched movies she couldn't see or hear


                                        or understand


on the La-Z-Boy that would soon hoist
        her to high heaven
in a far too comfortable throne of death,
        a vaguely capricious catafalque, singing
Goliath silence, swallowing her final breath with leather lips.


        It's true I can't sleep, I'm constantly rewriting my last words,
trying to nail a final epilogue
        perhaps best left to silence,
like the hound and those acorns of tragedy
        softly staring into the finality of forever,
a wedding dance with eternity,
        cauterized in the cerebral cortex of I
                                the adopted father
listening to tongue kissing rain
                        weeping on the roof


untrimmed nails still drumming on the laminate floor
        her spirit still bowling through the halls at night
nailing mahogany pedestrians like a blind yellow cab.

Tragedy knights itself, quickly becomes

> the sainted,

> > the sublime,

> > > the sole inspiration,


sitting here in this candle light,

> low and sorrowful, my passion

far greater than over-prescribed

> pesticides can withstand, far greater

than pest control can massacre termites

> or ants or junebugs, far greater

than a warhead could depopulate

> the Earth, far greater

than the toll and howl of severed species

> of humanities ceaseless conniption, hence the bottle of

Jack resigned to the nightstand;

> I'd like to stick a tattered rag inside,

hear the growl of a zippo striking flint,

> let the grief stricken crash fill the fuselage of my heart,

my face pieced together by firelight,

> think Poe at a lectern lamenting for dear Lenore.

# Funfair Parking Lots

Alec Montalvo

A Ferris wheel pirouetted around your pupils
from a distance and you didn't want to miss it
from the rain. You became the freight train
piloted off the rails, crashing parking lot puddles
with your steel legs, strutting past the lamp posts
lit with the lunar beams of disaster that have
enveloped our lives. You landed arms wide
into the wooden fence that separated us from
the carnival. Incandescent blues and reds
dragged lazily across the bridge of your nose,
we palmed our pockets flat in the dark, while
our eyes were like globe lights floating high
above the park that night.

# *Inman Park*

Kateland Leveillee

She is never what you want when you need her.
She never pacifies you.
She never calms your burning heart.
She lets it play on like a record.

She is lovely
until you want her,
gentle until you need her,
untouchable despite
her pulchritude.

And you love her,

though she is choosy with
moments she loves you back.

She wants you and all your artistry, then
resents you for touching
her with painted hands.

She wants you without wanting your parts.

You go on meds to calm your fears.
She leaves you for becoming

      less passionate.

# +anubis/-anubis

George L Stein

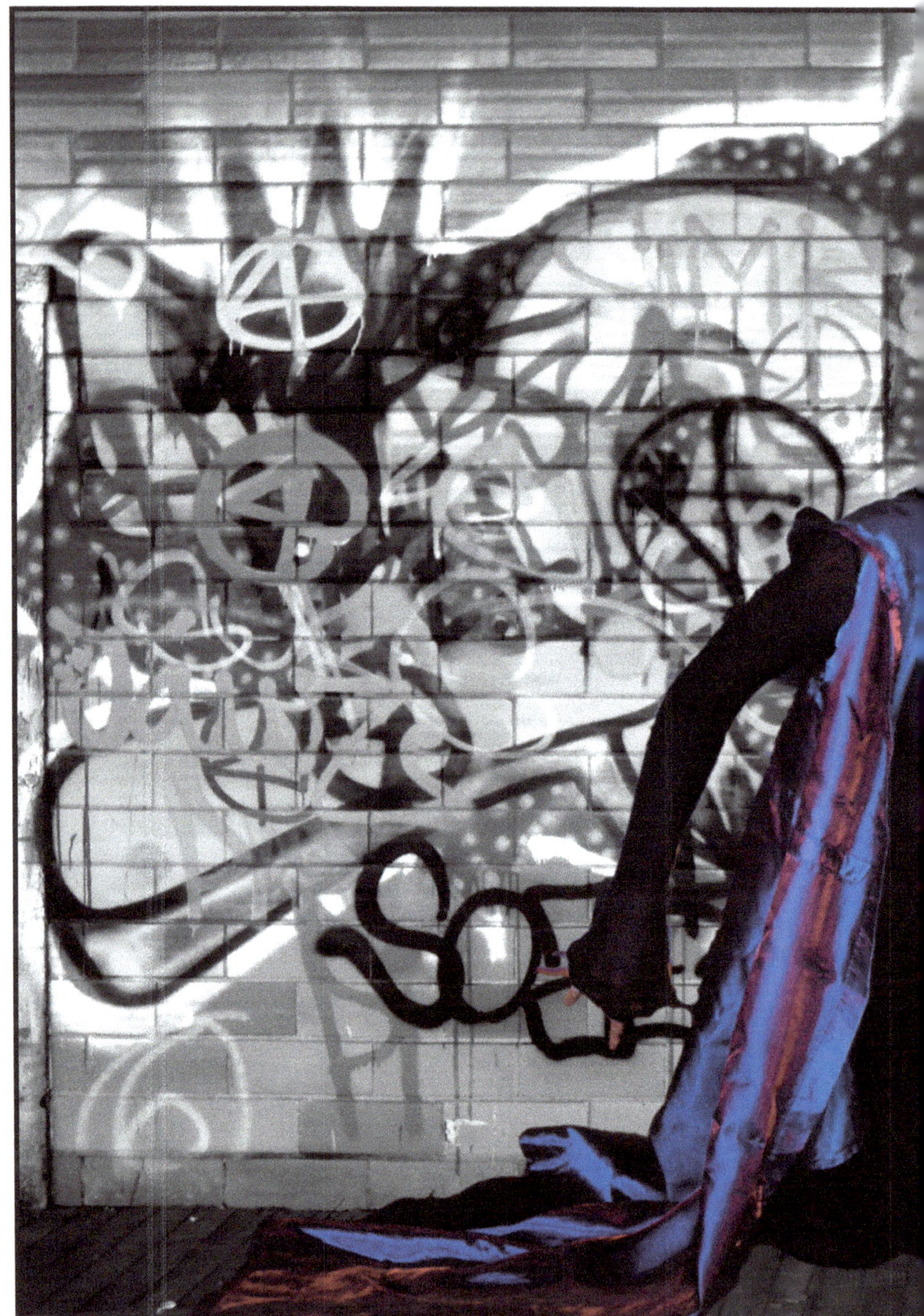

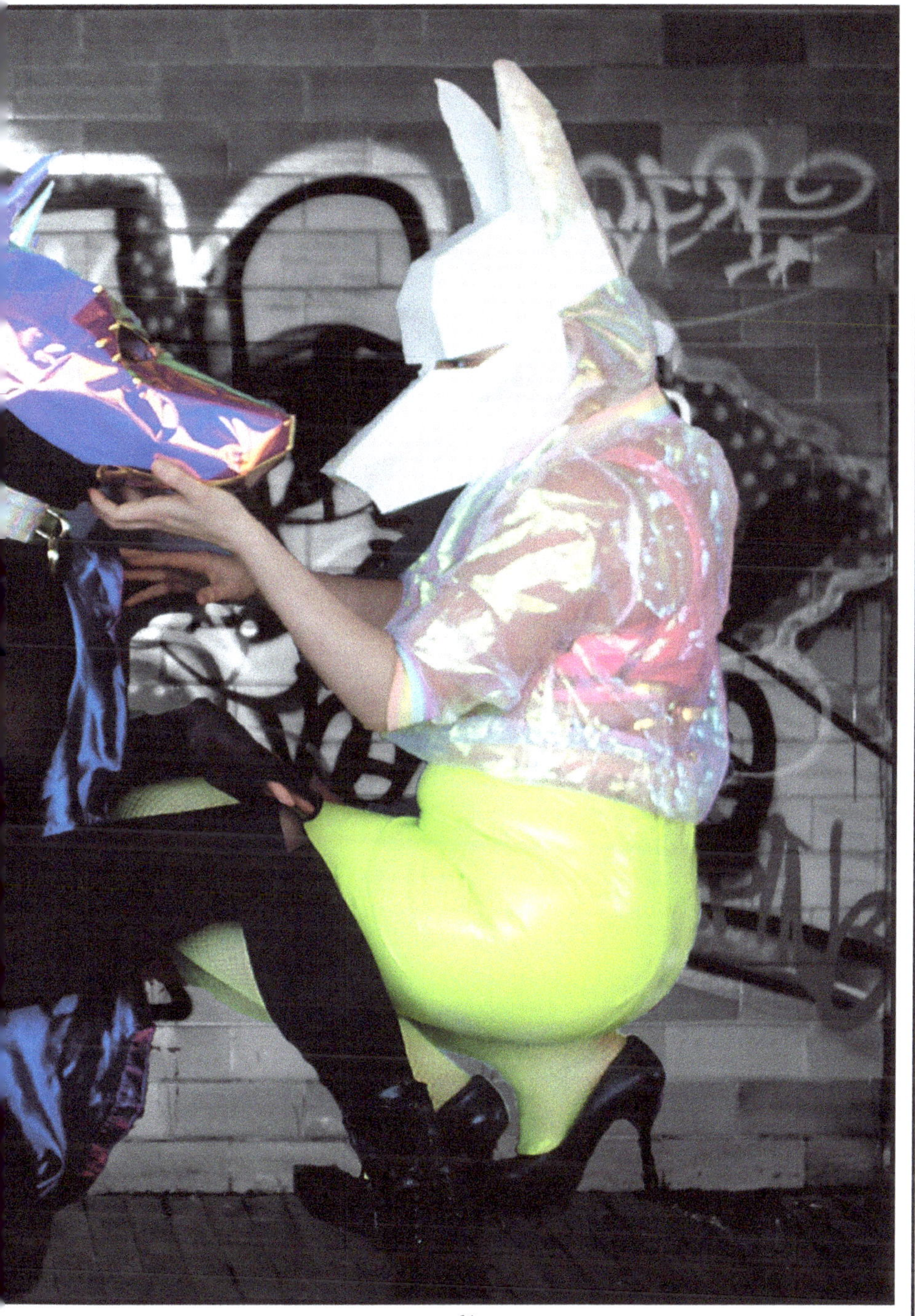

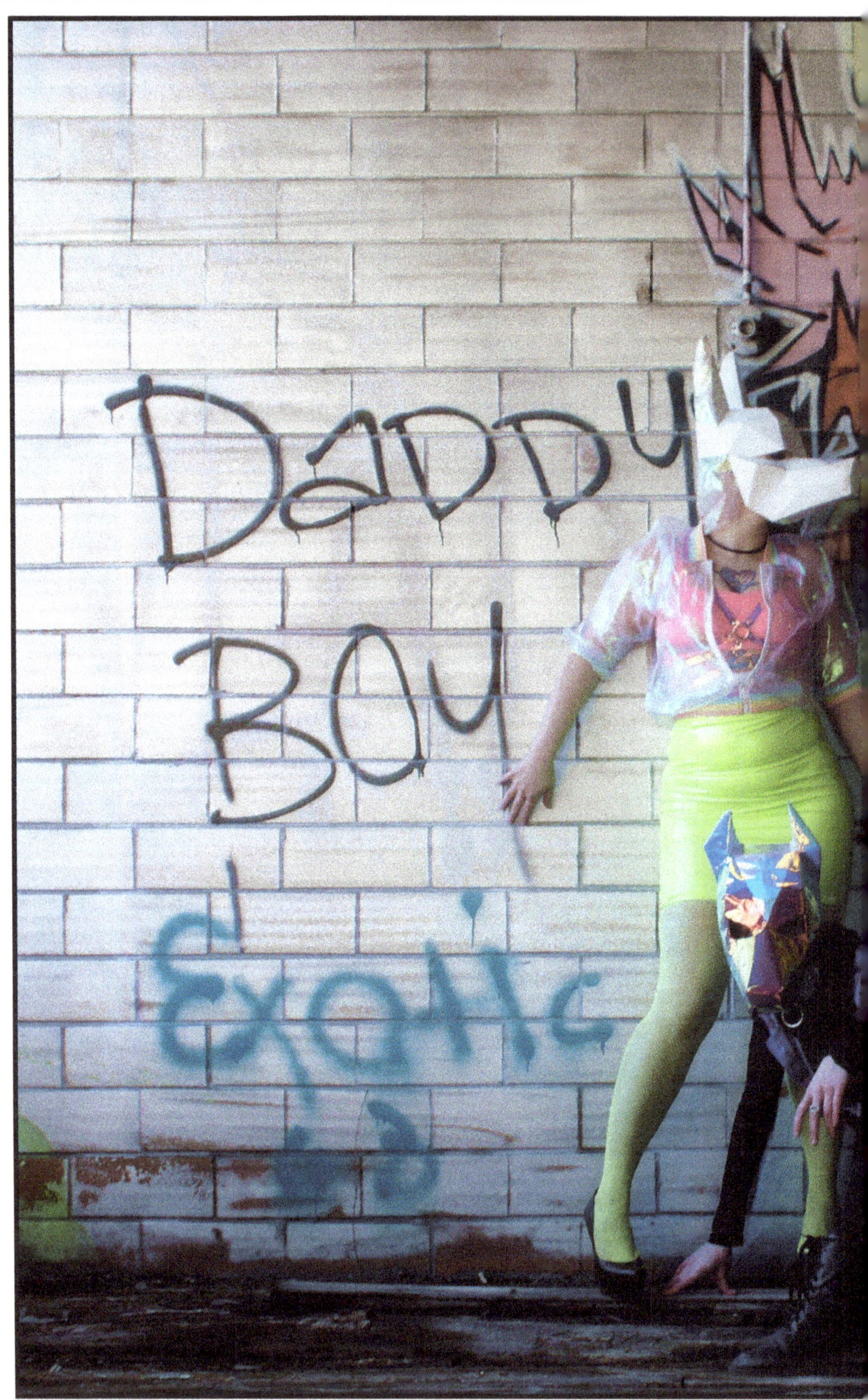
Daddy
Boy
Exotic

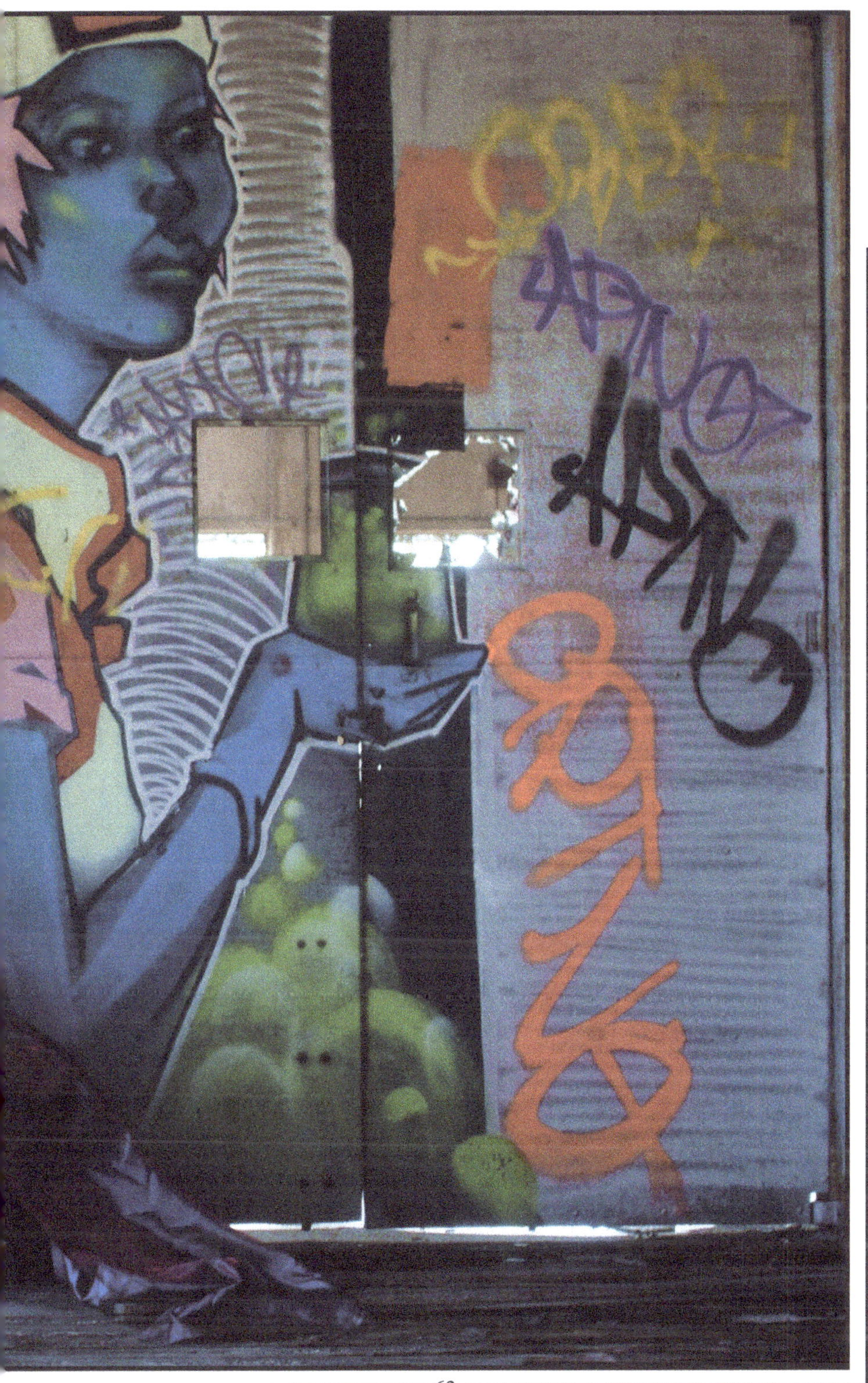

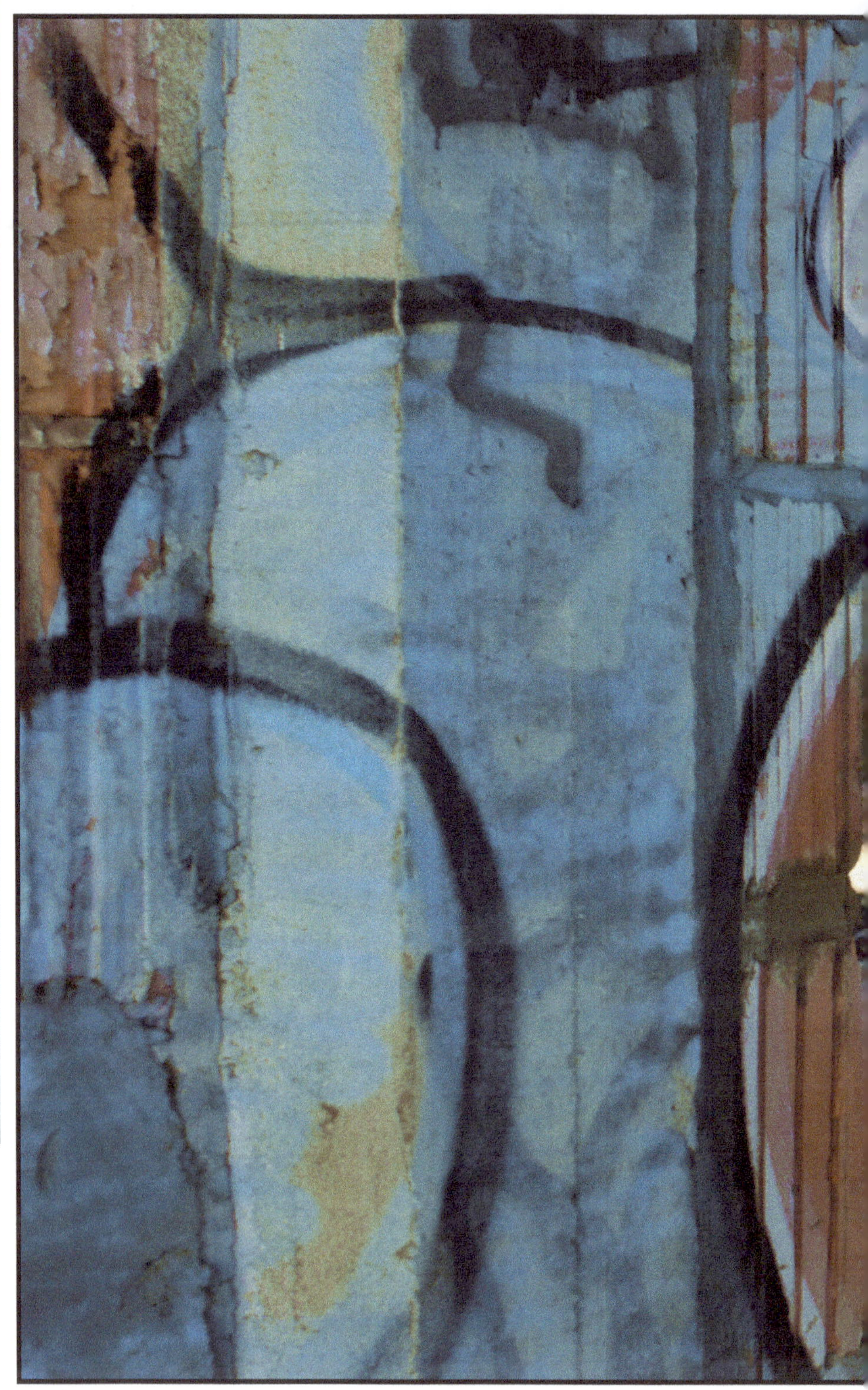

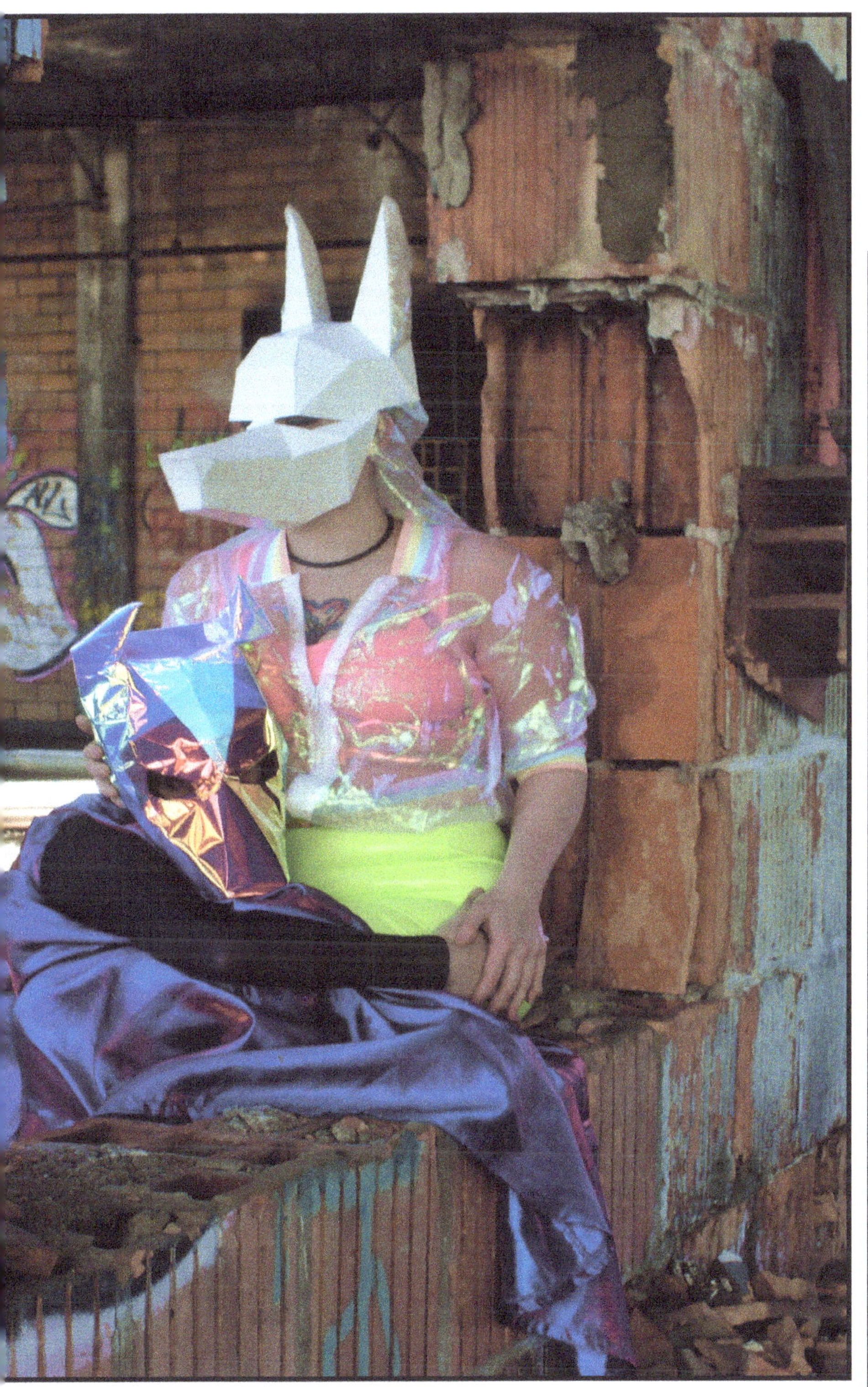

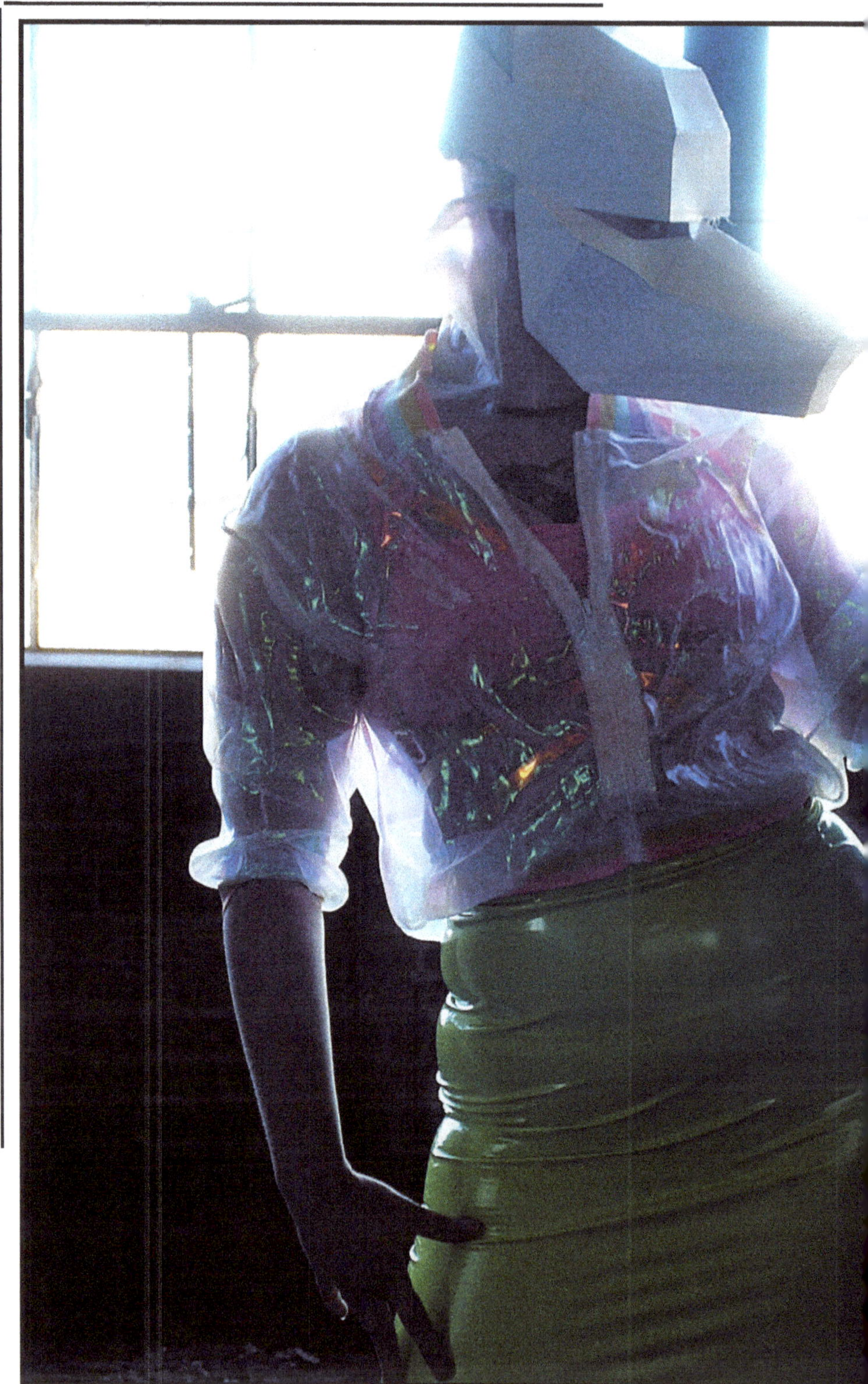

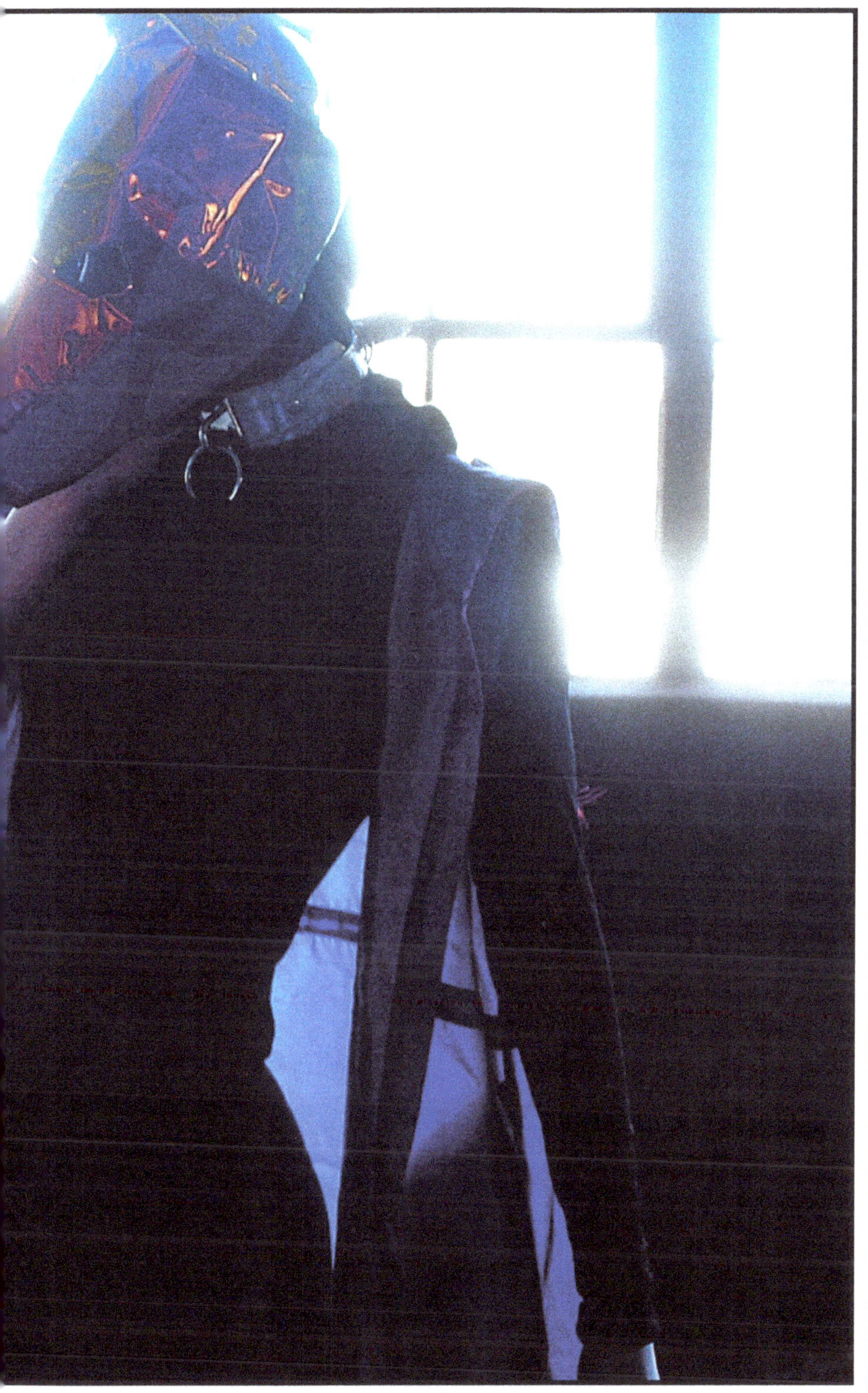

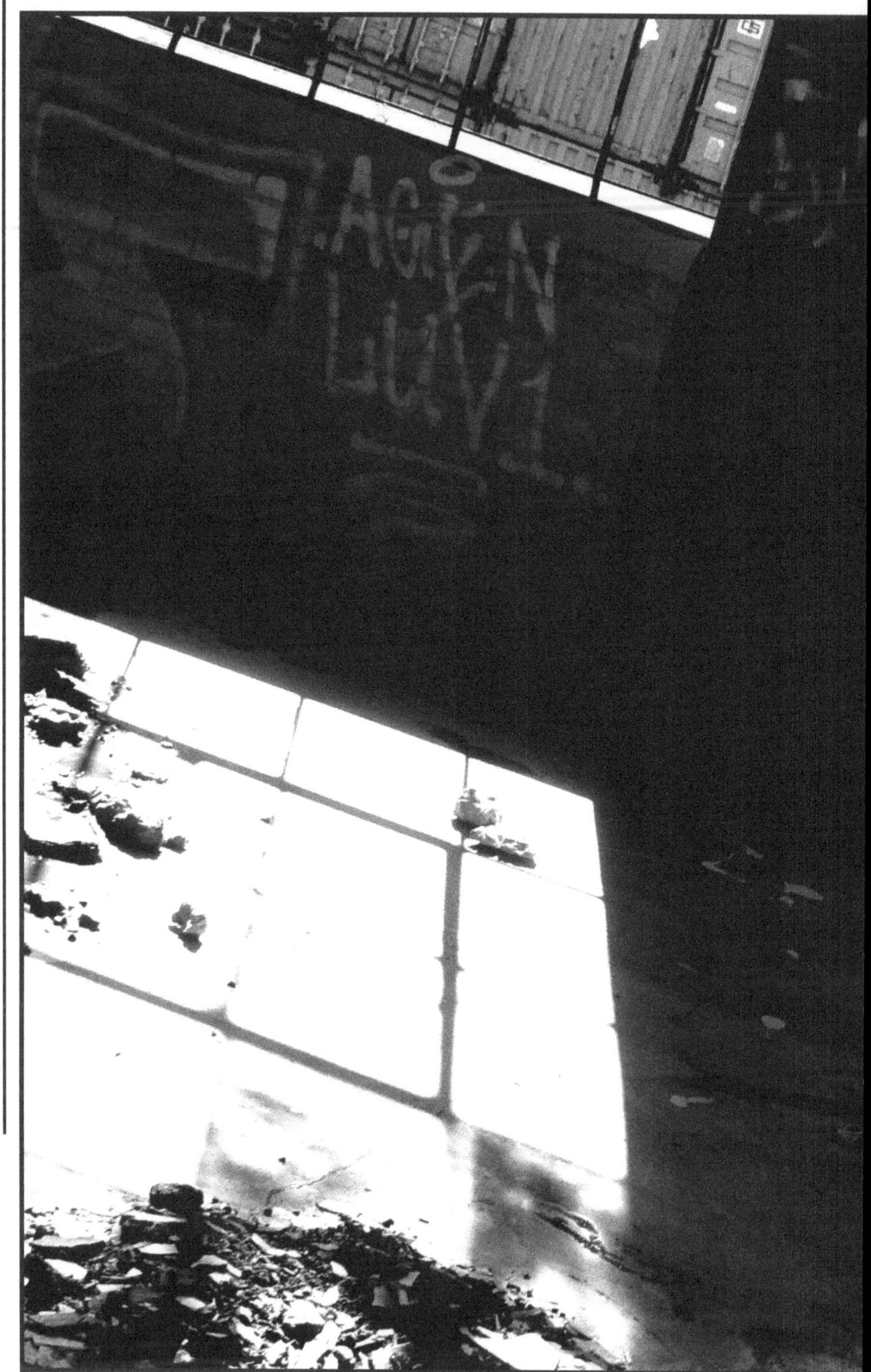

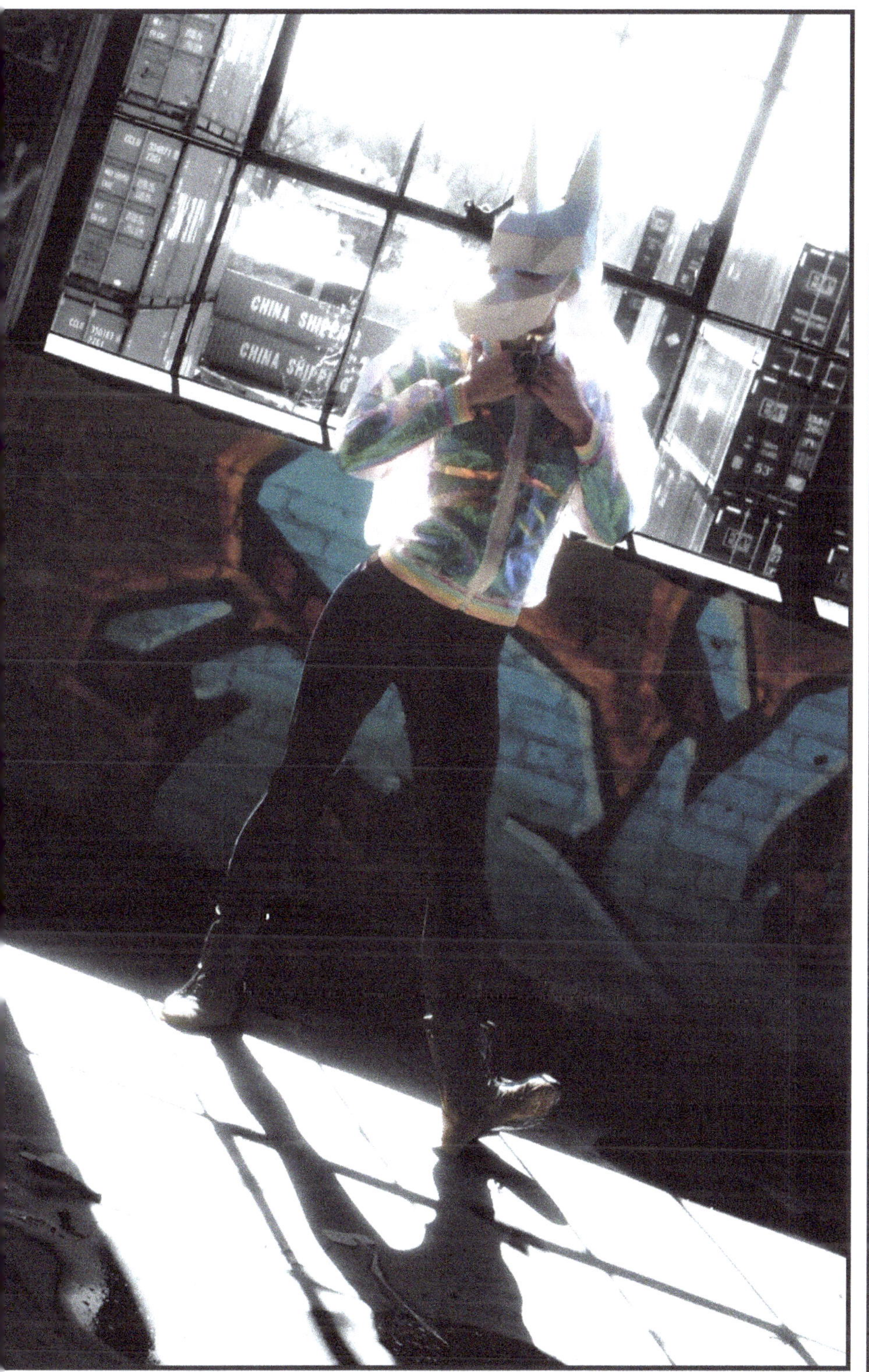

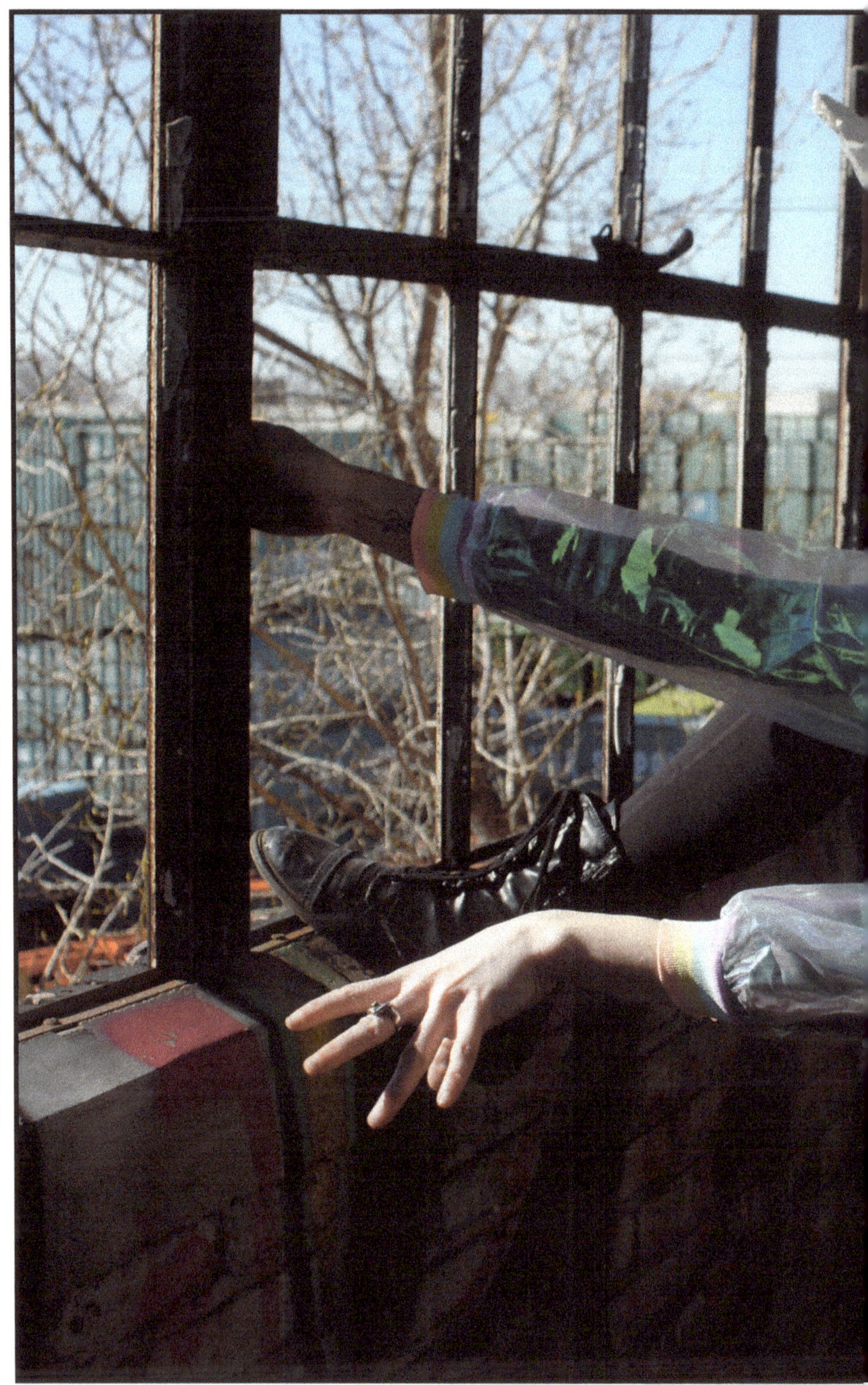

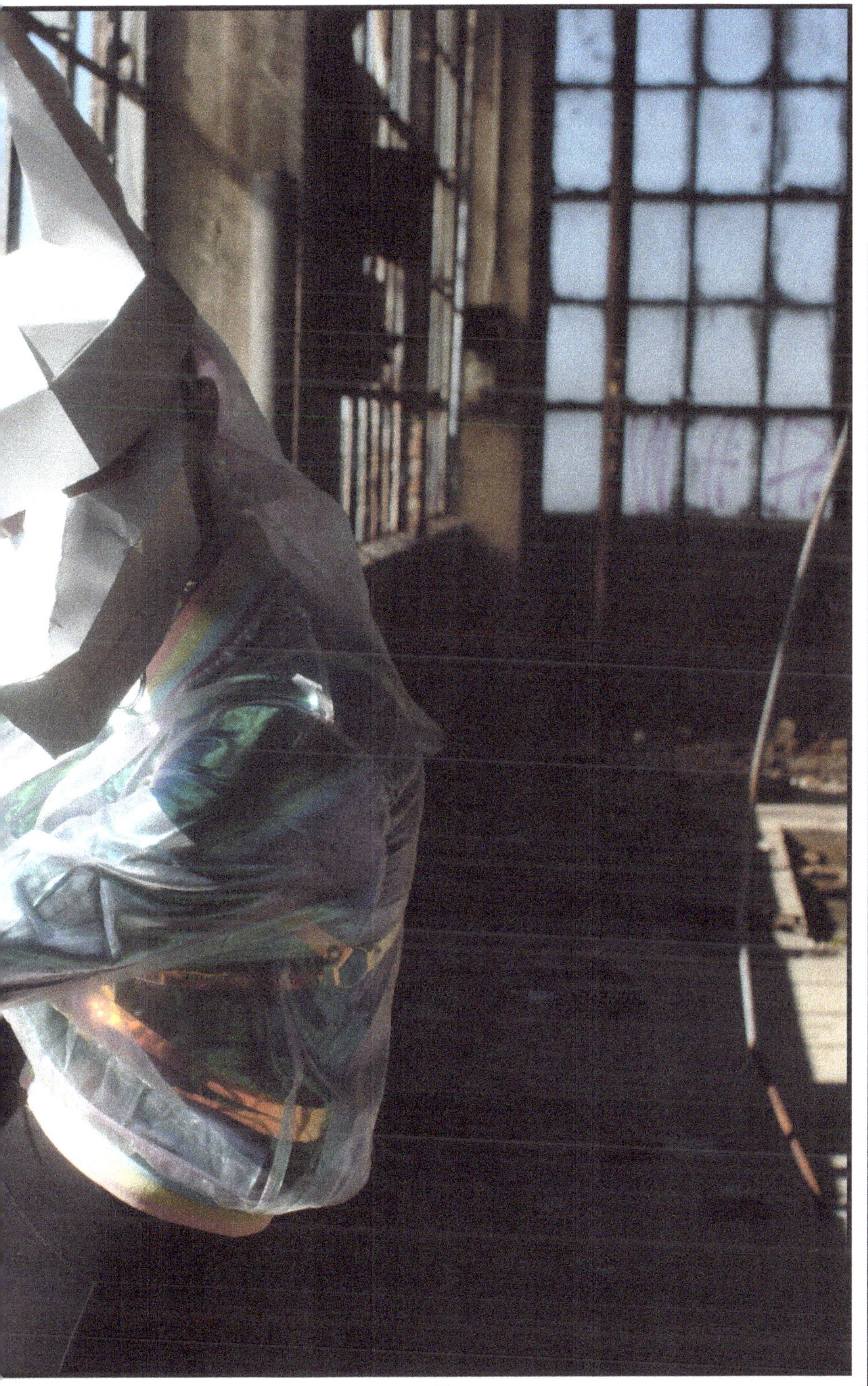

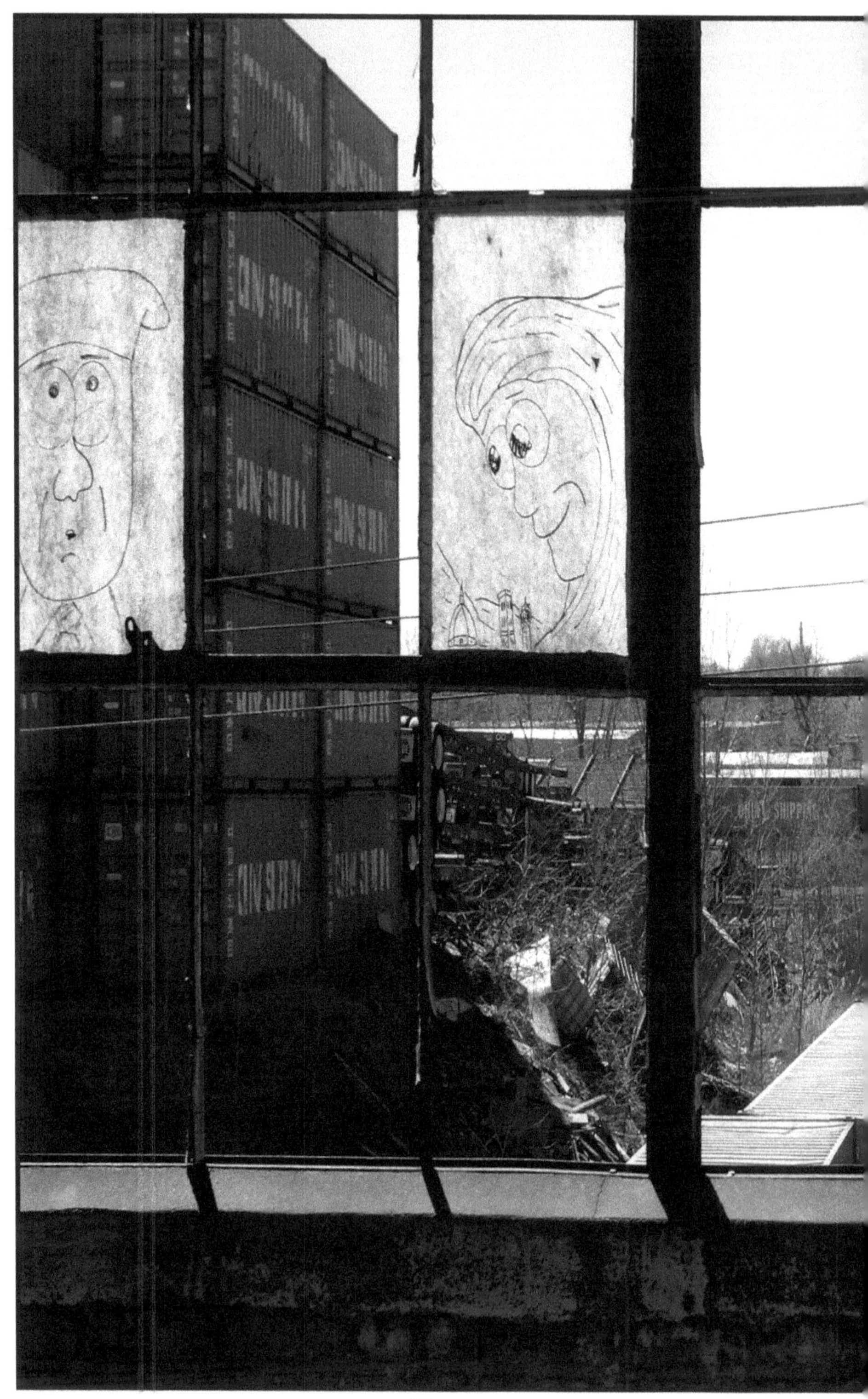

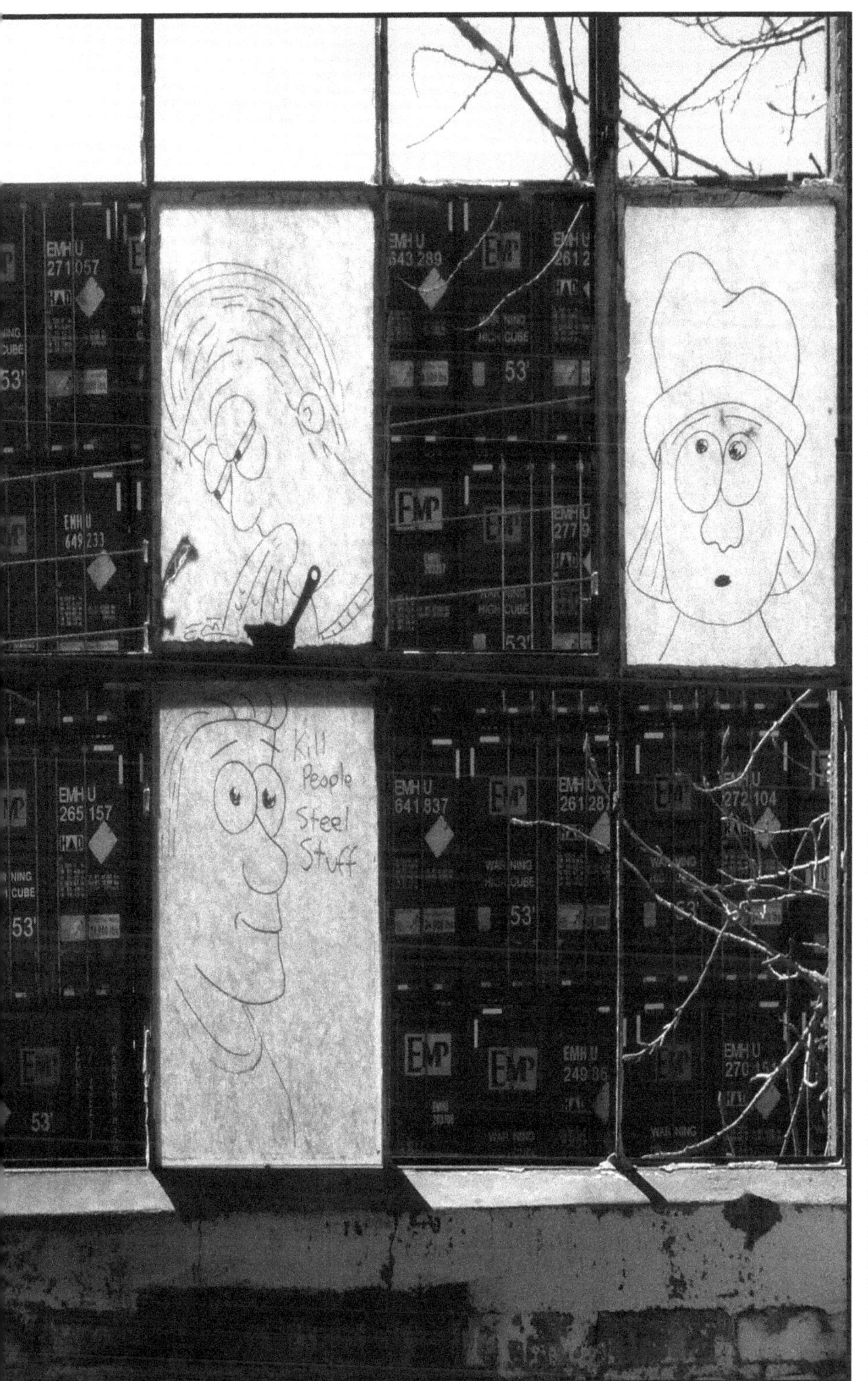
Kill
People
Steel
Stuff

# Losing The Bonus

Mark Reasoner

"Where's the spare magazine for my Glock nine mil?" Doug Meyer asked as he organized his pack for the day.

"Probably in the safe," his wife, Connie, replied. "I think you put it there after re-loading it."

Doug found what he needed right where his wife suggested. He stuffed it into an outside compartment.

"Thanks, babe," he said, kissing Connie goodbye. "I've got to go."

"Stay safe," Connie said.

Doug tossed his backpack onto the passenger seat of his Chevy Impala, started the car and backed out of his driveway. He turned on NPR for the thirty minute drive to Nugent High School where he taught Social Studies and Government.

He parked in his usual spot, shouldered his pack and made sure the pistol was set on his hip. All good. Approaching the building, he ran the usual gauntlet of students hanging out before the morning bell. He saw several students suddenly drop cigarettes or joints, crushing them underfoot.

*Some things never change*, he thought, smiling. Recreational marijuana might now be legal in the state, but all smoking was prohibited on school grounds. Not that this stopped anyone.

As he opened the steel door, Cliff Kramer, one of his fifth period students, came up.

"Hey, Mr. Meyer," the young man said, "Check this out." The teenager reached into his bag and pulled out a large handgun by the barrel. Cliff handed the shiny piece to Meyer.

"Sweet," Meyer said, turning in over in his hands. "M1911A, right?"

"Right," Cliff said, "I got it from my grandfather. Got a question, though, how do you carry it easily? Thing weighs a ton."

"Check old war films," Meyer said, "Most times, soldiers carried it strapped to the right hip, like old west gunslingers."

Meyer gave the pistol back and walked into the school. As he strode down the hall to his classroom, he caught snatches of typical high school conversation.

"...Needs to keep his hands off me, or I'll..."

"...Don't believe Timmy actually took that shot..."

"...Oh gross! Eww..."

"...Have you seen the new Beretta nines they're selling at the shop?"

Meyer took notice of two students close to his room.

"I don't want to talk about it," a short brown-haired girl said. "I don't want to talk to you, either."

"You better talk to me, bitch," the taller boy replied, "I can make you."

The boy pulled a thirty-eight chief special from his jacket and shoved the barrel under the girl's chin. Meyer moved over to shut the confrontation down.

"That's enough, Mr. Vinton! You know the rules. Put that thing away or take it outside. Shootouts are not allowed in the halls."

When Jerry Vinton shoved his pistol harder against the girl's jaw, Meyer reached to his right hip and drew his nine millimeter Glock pistol. He pointed it at the boy's head.

"Now, Jerry, or I will shoot. I'm allowed, you know."

Vinton looked at Meyer, seeing the teacher's determined look. The young man lowered his weapon and returned it to his pocket.

"This isn't over, c**t," he mumbled as he moved off.

"Thanks, Mr. Meyer," the girl said.

"Do I want to know what's going on?" Meyer asked.

"No."

The bell rang and everyone moved toward their classrooms.

Such was the typical day's opening at Nugent High. With everyone carrying handguns and authorized to use them with discretion and proper cause, each morning brought the possibility of confrontation. The students were more restricted than the teachers, but situations were known to escalate and teachers were allowed to use deadly force to contain things. Paperwork, though, was extensive in those cases, so everyone tried to avoid it.

# THE VEGANS OF ENGLAND COUNTY

John David Morgan

Megan Erin Johnson was a vegan.

A 70-year-old vegan. In England County, Kentucky. In 1976.

Not likely.

But that's exactly what she was. Actually, she was the second vegan in the small Kentucky county.

The first of those rascals was Dr. Bradford Winslow.

Folks said that Dr. Winslow had moved to England County from Idaho, or Montana, or maybe Wyoming, at least someplace out there west of the Mississippi. No one knew exactly why he left the west, but it was said he settled in England County because he liked the mountains.

The dentist did not hit it off initially with the good people of England County. For one thing, his first name was "Bradford", and no man or woman in Appalachia would ever name their boy that. To them, Bradford was a type of pear tree that bloomed for about a week in the spring.

For another thing, the locals thought him uppity. He talked about how great it was fishing for trout back there in Colorado, or New Mexico, or Utah, or wherever it was. He had the nerve to say in public that trout fishing was better than catching a big mouth bass or a muskie. Few people ever actually saw him go fishing, and those that did never reported him catching anything bigger than a blue gill. And, whatever he did catch, he always let it loose.

What sort of fool would go to all the trouble of catching a fish, and then let the durn thing loose?

But, several of the livelier folks in town did start to come to his defense, once it was known he was fond of moonshine. And as health plans slowly improved, and more union workers started receiving dental benefits, the town gradually accepted him.

Sort of.

It was Dr. Winslow that had personally instructed Megan Erin in the joys of veganism.

In fact, the Widow Johnson (as Megan Erin was now called) had a very close and personal relationship with the good dentist. In Noah's will, all of the Johnson assets were in a living trust for his widow, with the condition that if she remarried, the assets would immediately transfer fifty-fifty to a coal miners' charity and the University of Kentucky. Several lawyers were hopeful that this would happen, since they either knew of, or could easily create, a coal miner's charity that would need a great deal of their legal expertise.

Dr. Winslow had brought a small fortune (the key word being small) with him from the west. But it was nothing near the king's ransom left to Megan Erin by the strip-mine owner Noah. As a result, the Widow Johnson was frequently seen going into Dr. Winslow's office at all hours, and the good doctor was even known to make house calls for dental emergencies to his favorite patient.

This caused a great deal of talk with the professional gossipers in England County, a "professional" being defined as them that spent more than three-fourths of their free time in that activity.

Megan Erin was a favorite topic as far away as Lexington, where the Logan Shelby stock broker Worth Berry was known to say: "that Widow Johnson over in England County is what they call a vegan."

And when the listener asked the question of what exactly a vegan actually was, Worth would respond:

"I ain't exactly sure, but I expect it's a might like a foot-washing Baptist, only it's about the mouth. Cause it's a shore-enough fact, that Widow Johnson has the cleanest teeth in all of eastern Kentucky."

# Experiments

Joe Hedges

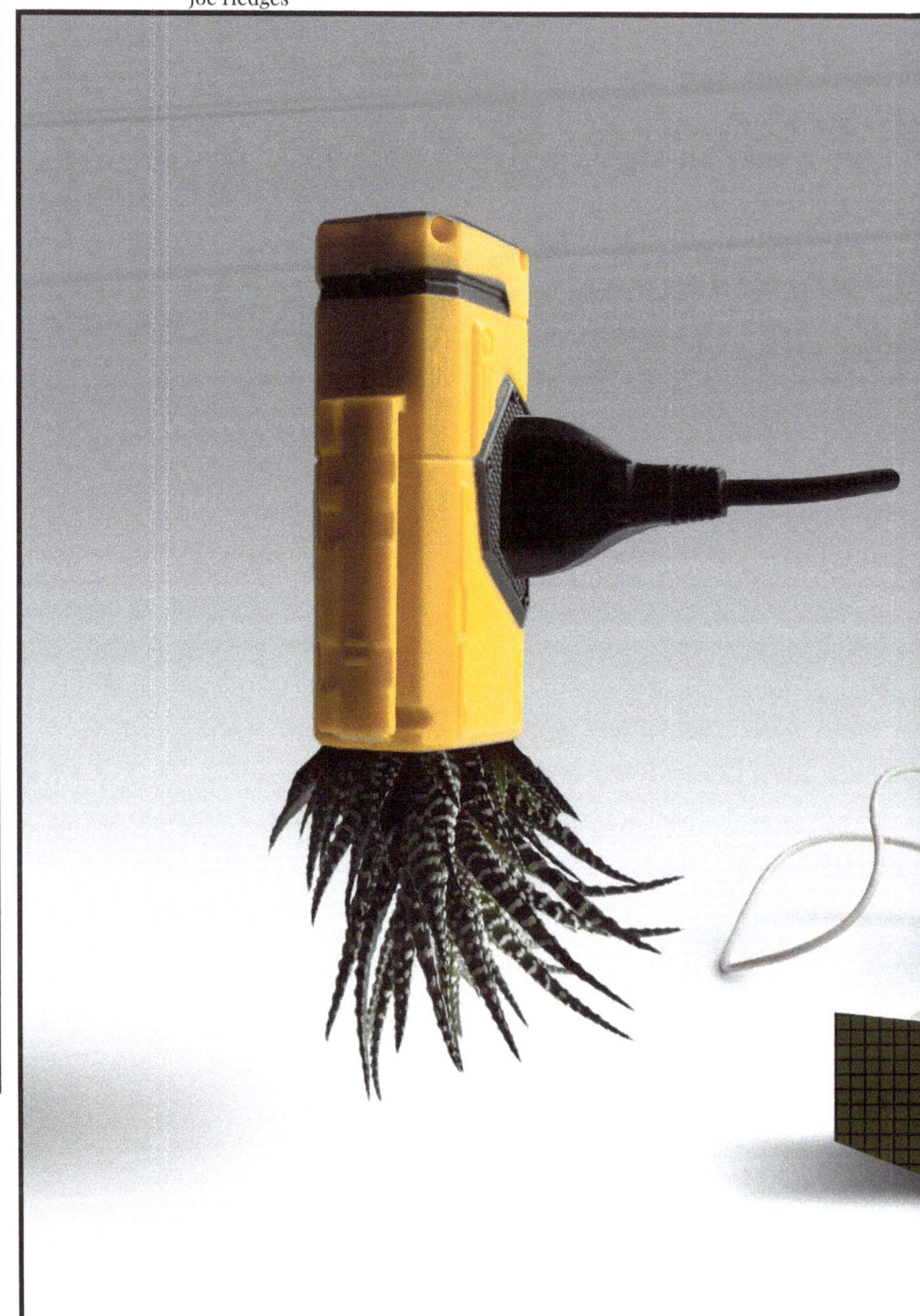

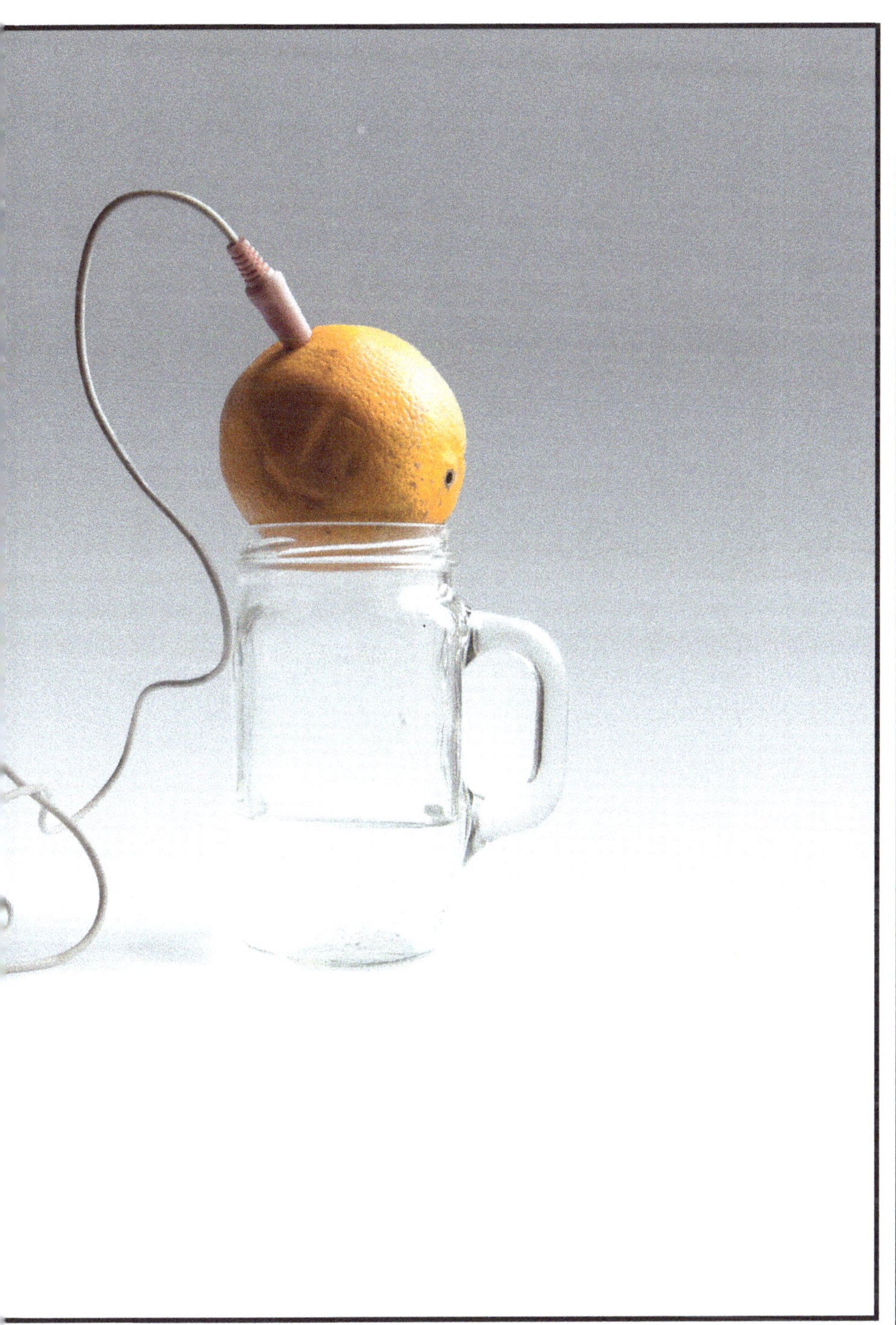

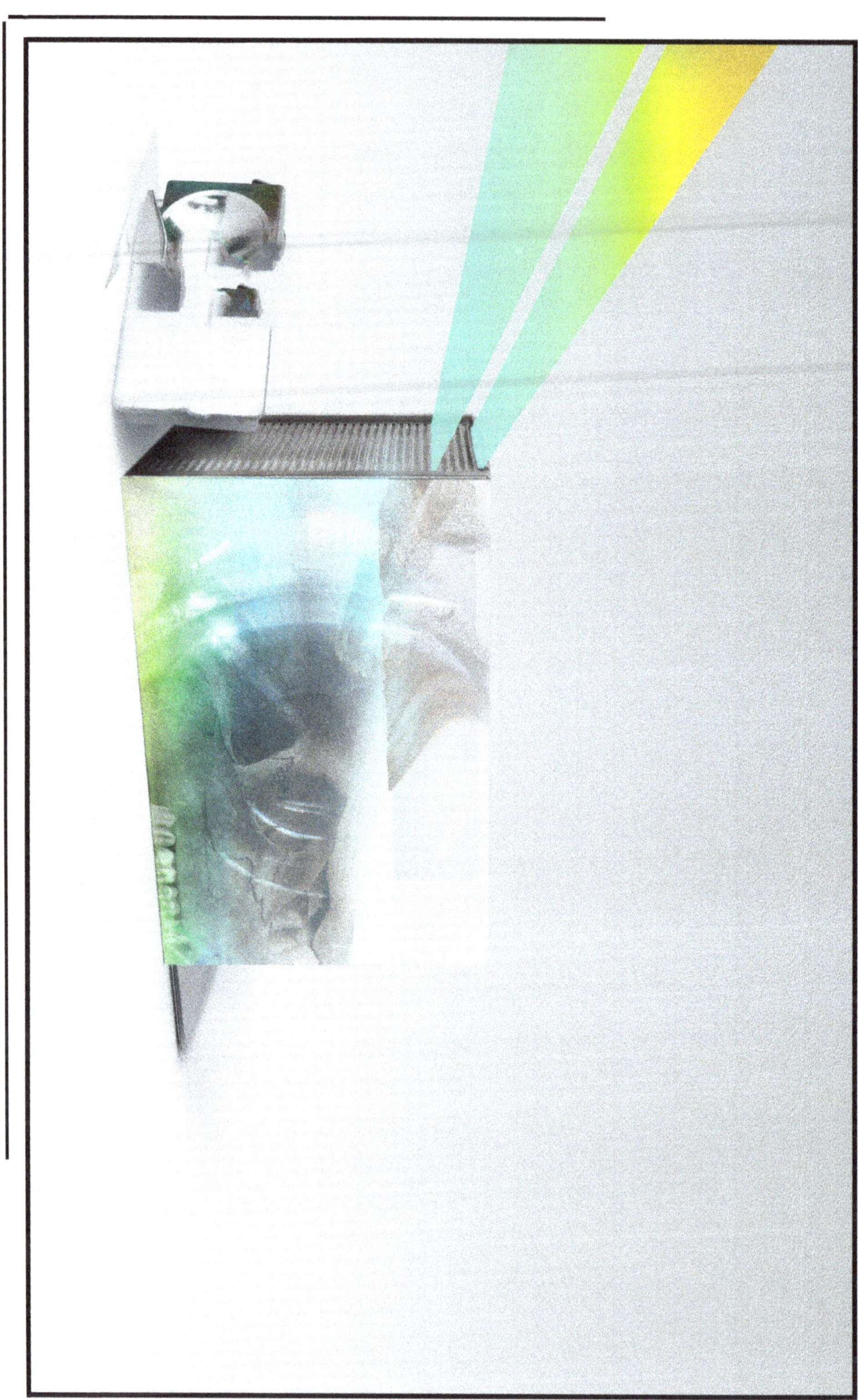

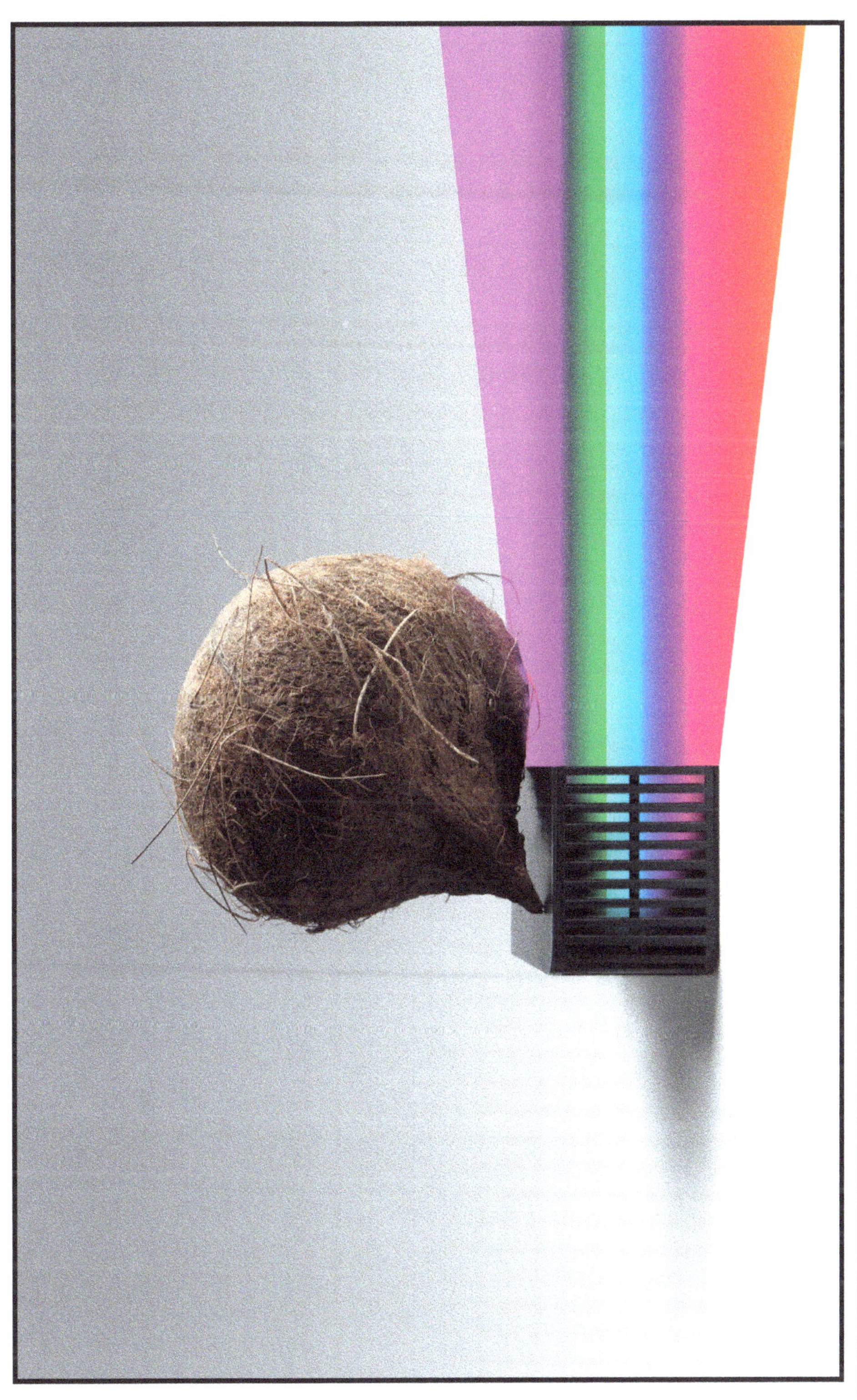

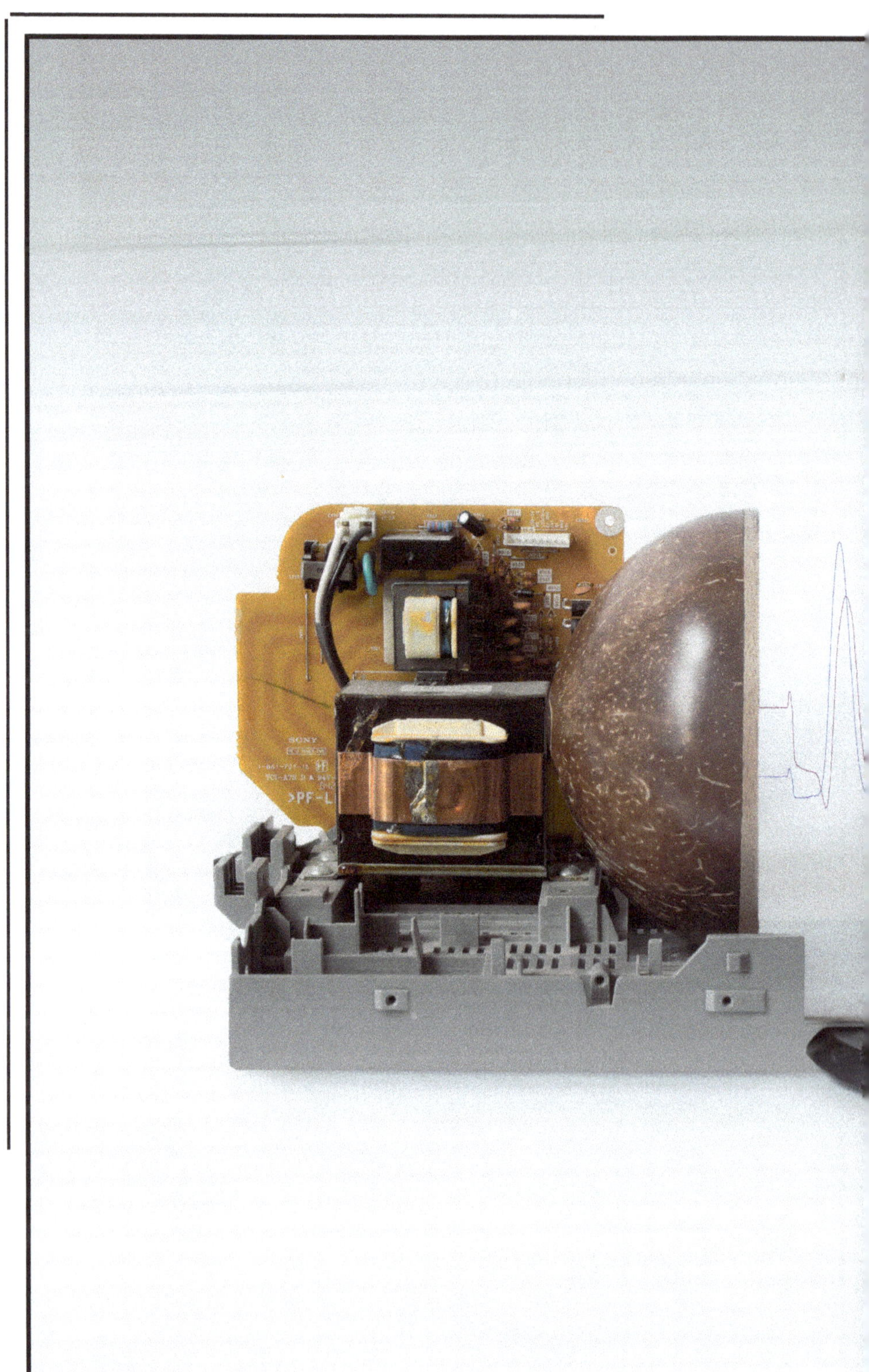

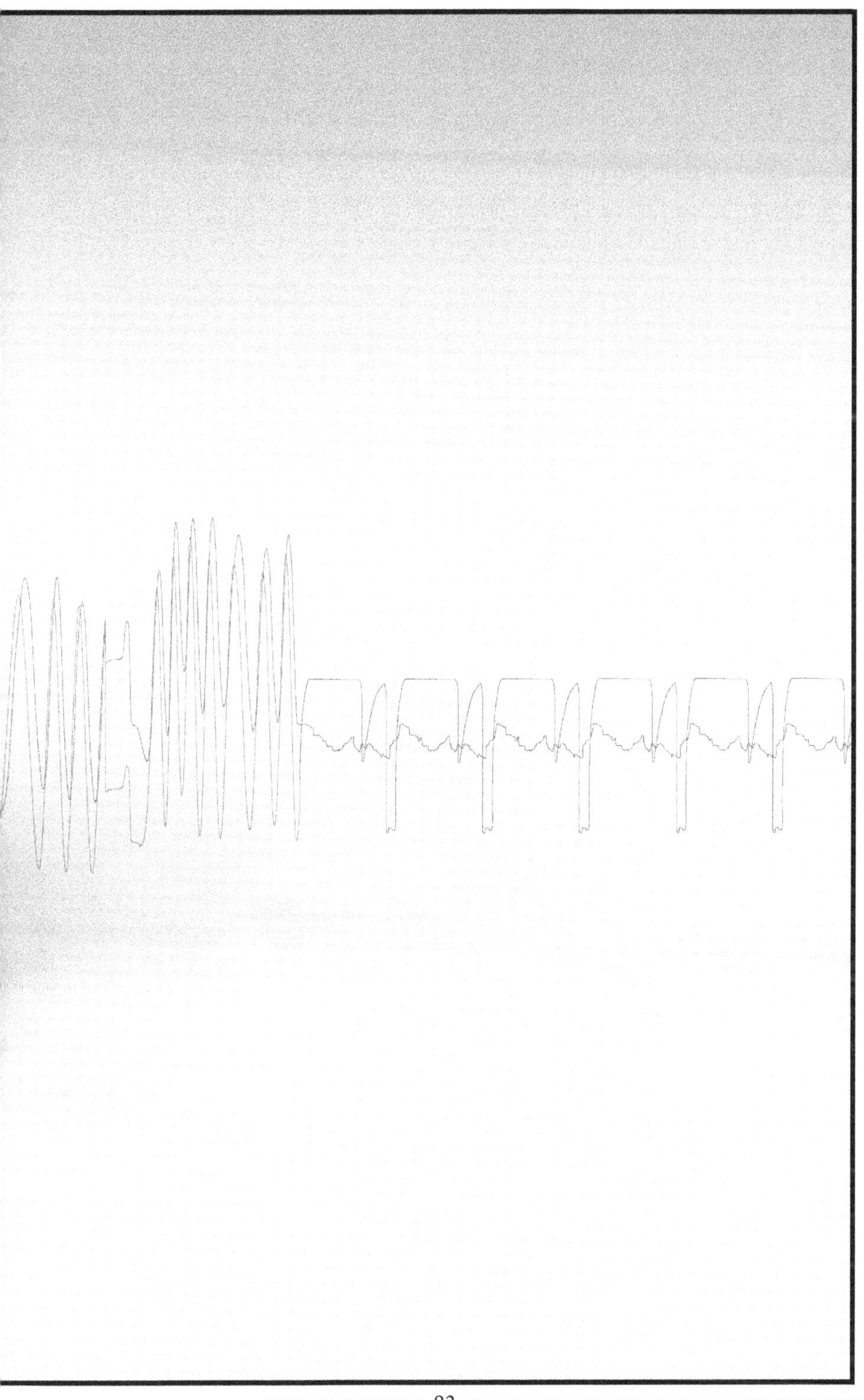

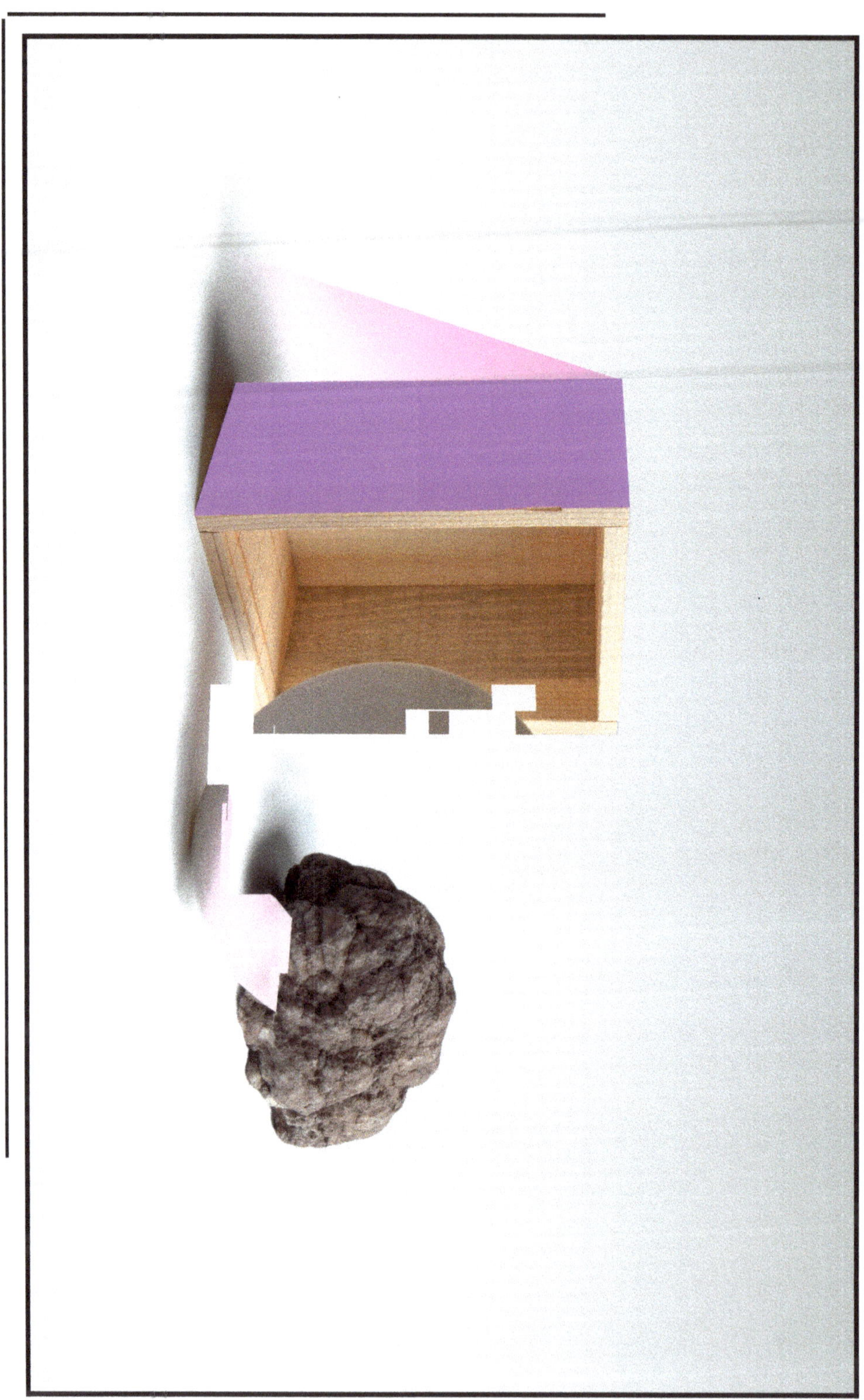

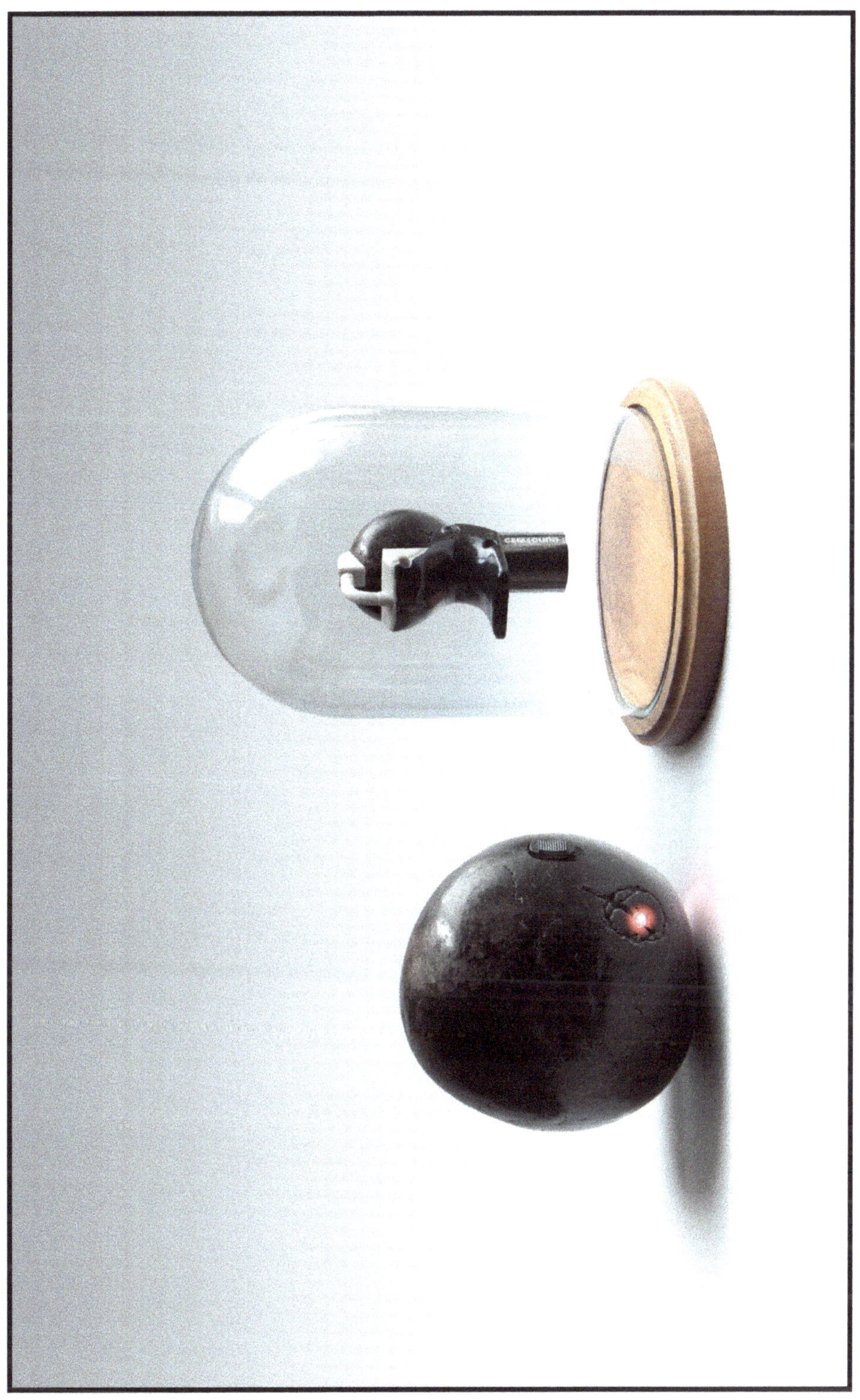

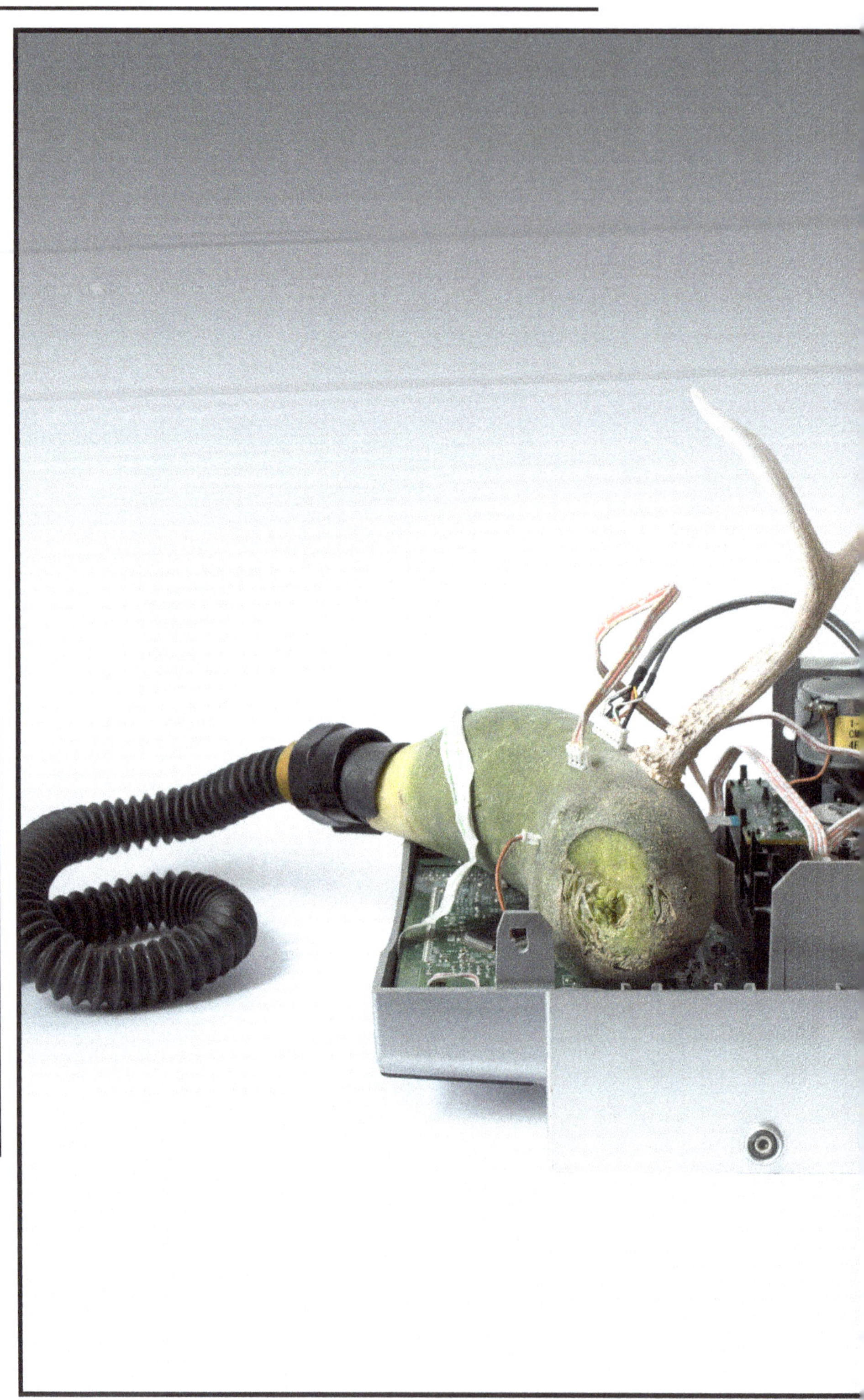

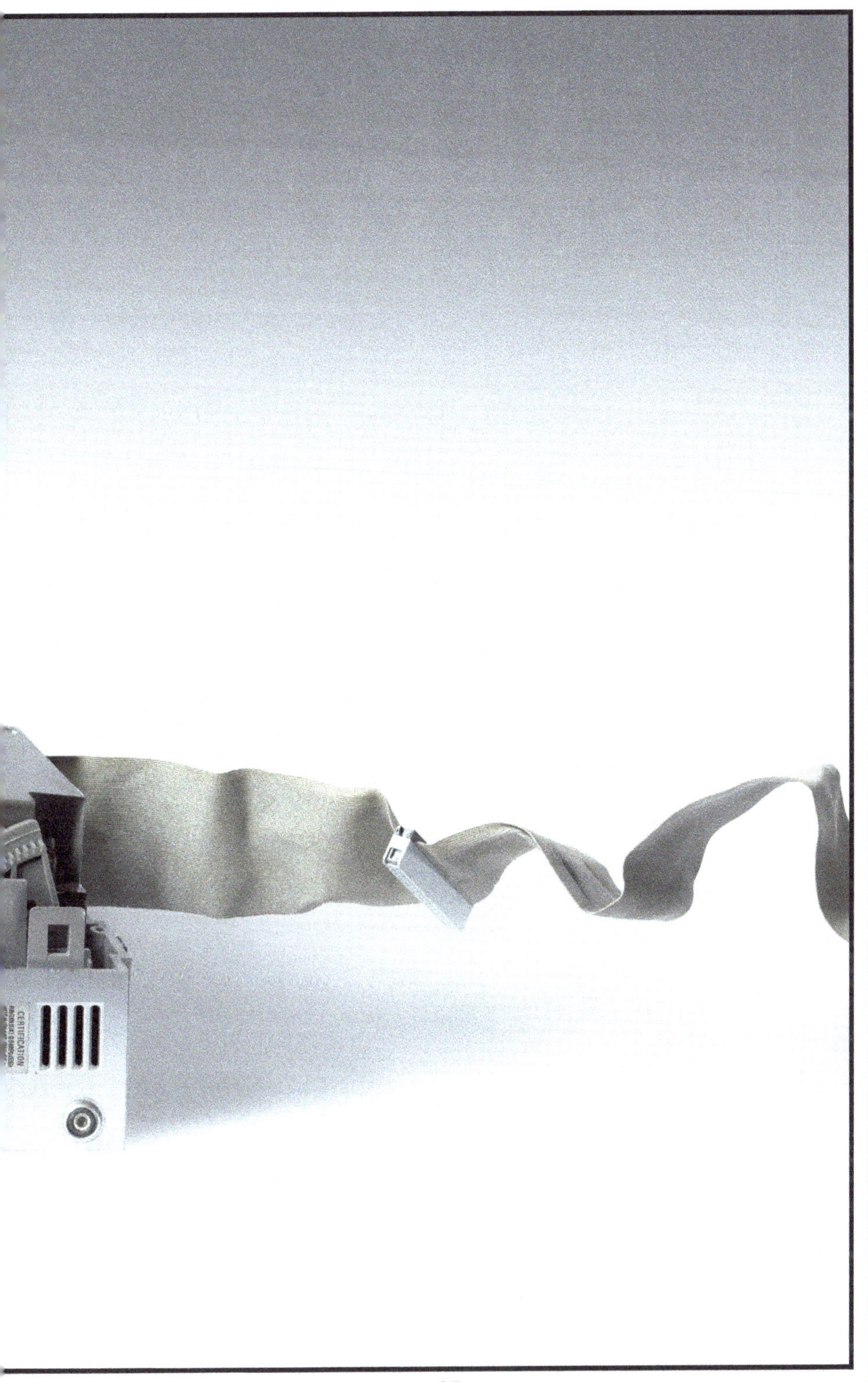

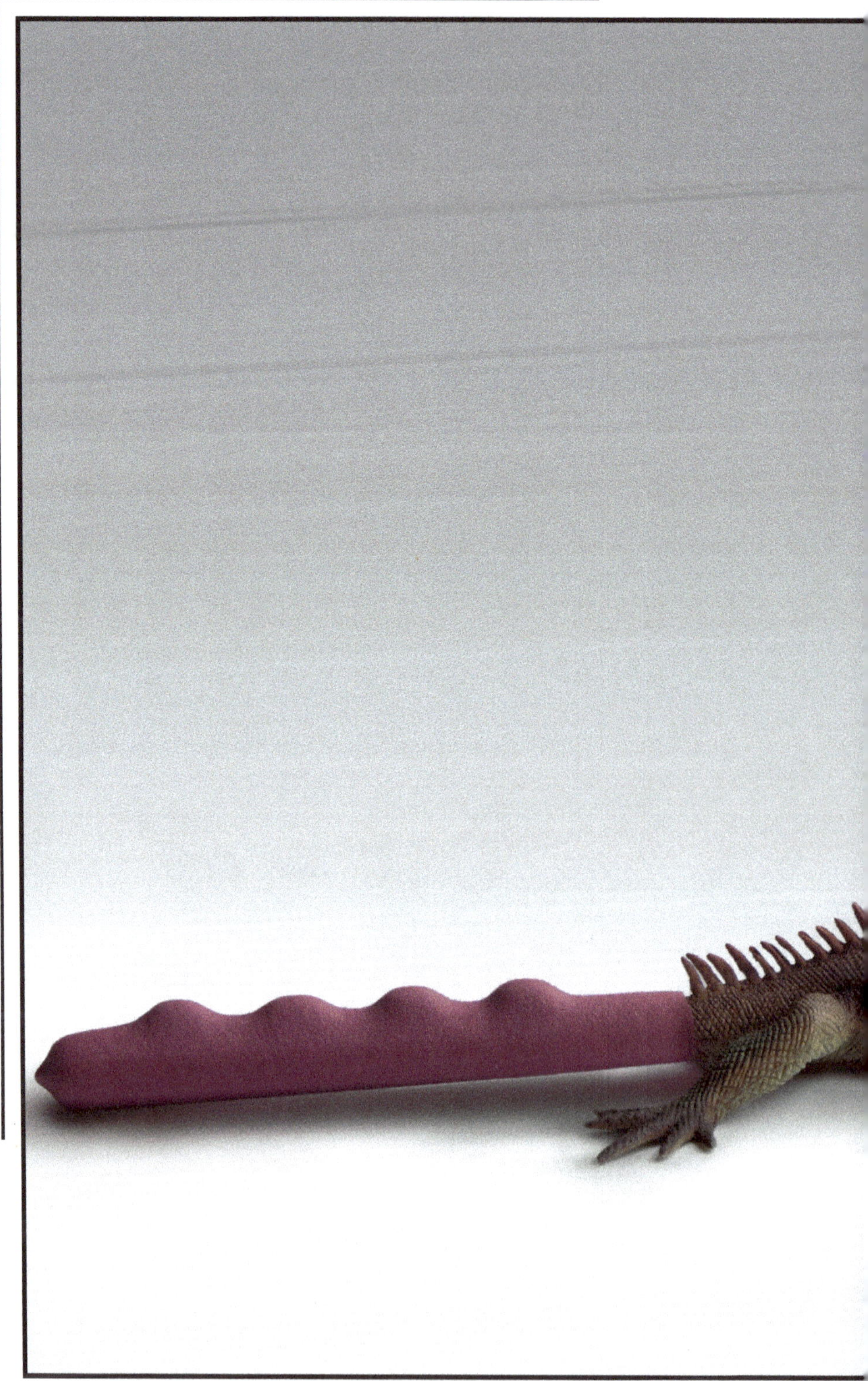

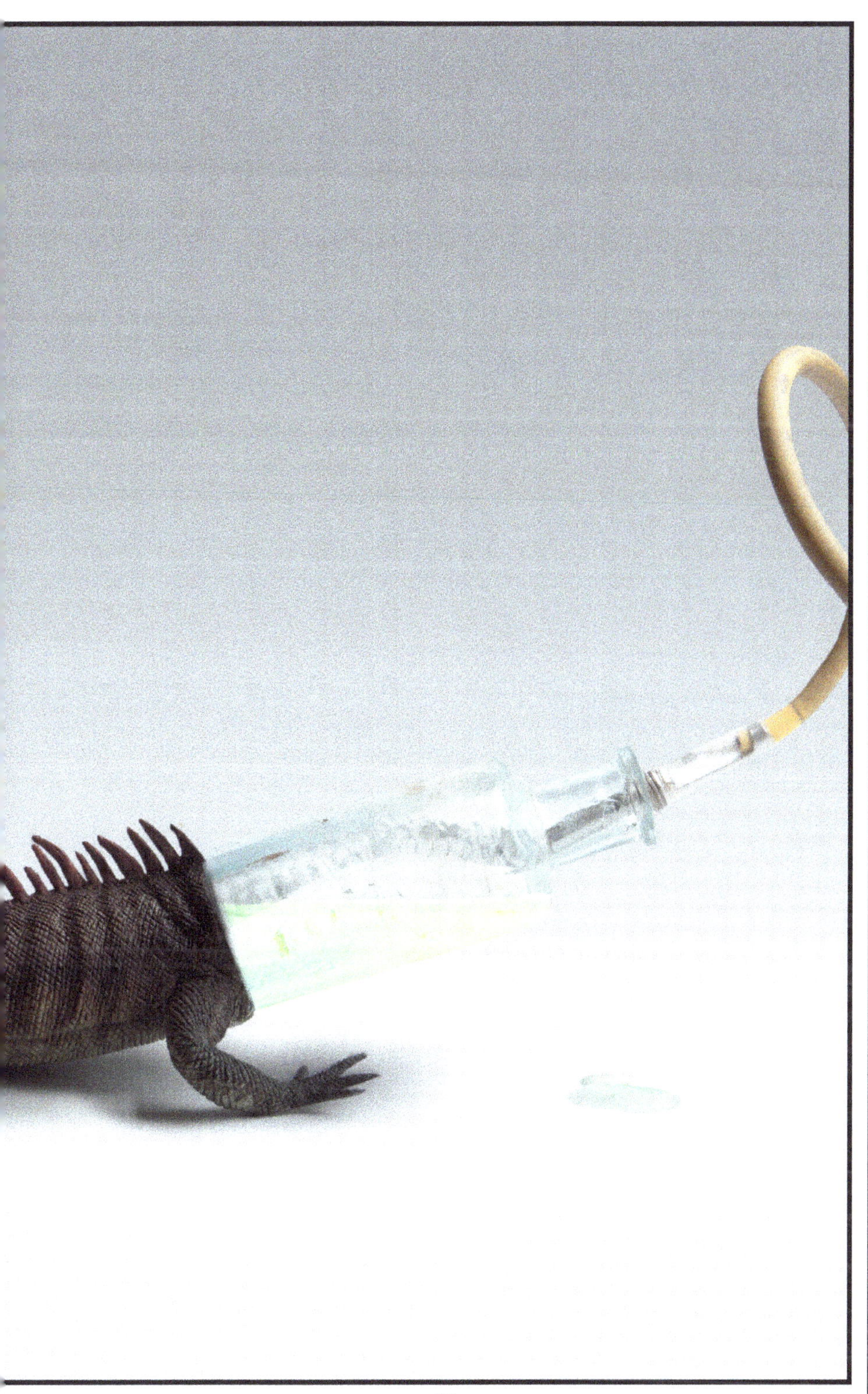

# Trauma World Park - "We Make the Tragic!"

Jennifer Dines

A Special Message from Your Trauma World Hosts:
This guidebook was created to support you in navigating our park. We have included information on all you might need to navigate the most exciting attractions, scrumptious dining choices, and retail therapy opportunities of Trauma World Park. We wish you luck as you descend into the circles of your personal history.

### CineTrauma

Relive the memories of yesteryear in this 3-D montage guaranteed to trigger you over and over! Scenes include Dad flipping the dinner table causing a ceramic plate to chip your tooth — because you begged to attend that 7th grade sleepover — and Mom smashing up the piano with a hammer after accusing you of liking your piano teacher more than her.

### House of Tragic

A museum of miniature mementos of your parents' arguments. Family photos behind cracked glass, audio samples of swears and insults, and commemorative portraits of denial — all free of scratches, bruises, scowls, and tears.

### Pirates of Your Vulnerability

 An ensemble cast of pirates and privateers inappropriately plunder the fragility of your budding adolescent sexuality. Villains include your guitar teacher and a rotation of adult men who hang out at the coffee shop where you work.

### Off the Edge of the Map Espresso Bar

Ash Marlboro Lights into a tiny cup of coffee as your seventeen-year-old self ponders where exactly your mother ran off with your sister when she left your father. And why she didn't provide you a phone number or a forwarding address.

### The Loose Cannon

Practice hitting the deck as your father fires off verbal ballistics that remind your early-twenty-something self  why you are "a little bitch who should mind your own business" — the precedent being a discussion about his health — his smoking, drinking, gambling, and spending time in the hospital and in jail.

### Terror Jets

Board our miniature fighter planes and endure our threatening skies. While all the other passengers smile and take photographs, you will experience violent shaking, profound nausea, and a pounding heart beat. This unforgettable experience is accompanied by an original Karlheinz-Stockhausen-inspired score of whirs, dings, and buzzes.

## The Hall of Lost Friendships

A dramatic presentation of former friends that you lost when you started binge drinking every night — each character offers detailed monologues of your self-destruction. Repeats every few months or so.

## The Weeping Cup Café

Order up a TraumaWorld souvenir mug and fill it with your own warm tears. Free refills.

## Carousel of Intergenerational Mental Illness

A showcase displaying a century of hard liquor, beer, wine, prescription painkillers, and flat-out psychosis. After the show, enjoy a complimentary consultation from a TraumaWorld Gentle Guide at guest services. Additional therapeutic services can be purchased for the rest of your life.

## Celestial Paradise

Ascend into tranquil skies accompanied by a TraumaWorld Gentle Guide. Float amongst the stars of faith, love, and hope.

## Phantom Mansion

Ghosts and goblins of your past rise from their graves at spookily uneven intervals. An exorcism at the end of each ride quells the spirits, but not for long.

## Guess What's Next!

A lot of construction — and destruction — is going on around TraumaWorld Park, so you'll have more reasons than ever to feel anxious, depressed, manic, suicidal, and maybe even temporarily stable. There is always room for you in the Mental Suffering Kingdom!

# Help! I was Supposed to Assassinate the Dark Sorcerer Kahn Huzbard but I Slept Through my Clepsydra's Alarm

Ed Scherrer

Big fuck up on my part, people. My damn clepsydra was supposed to sprinkle water onto my face and wake me up but the perfidious wizard Khan Huzbard sent an enchanted mongoose into my tent and the lanky animal's musk turned my face into a mask of insensate bronze (on which the tinkle of water had no perky effect). Only when the crimson light of dawn licks the crocodile's dagger, bestowed by the luminous Princess Kaur, can its curved blade effectively jugulate Huzbard and turn him into a writhing fount of gore. But according to the obelisk's shadow it's now—oh, fuck me, really? And by now Kahn Huzbard's scaly skin is surely as impermeable as his seven hearts are black and I'm pretty much SOL. Upon my albino camel I will fly to the catacombs and surely find that Kahn Huzbard has opened the gates of the shadow realm and fulfilled his terrible destiny. Sigh. I just hope one of my team members, maybe Karen—or the new guy, what's his name, he likes the Detroit Lions, Todd, got to the office on time and managed the presentation without me. Alas, according to their wretched soul-screams that burst from my enchanted talisman, I'm a real piece of shit that can't be counted on for anything.

# A MOST IMPORTANT MAN

*Pamela Sumners*

You think you don't know me, but you do.
I am Eliot's eternal snickering footman,
the Anti-Christ's Groom of the Stool.
My job lacks the refinement of a cabinet post,
but most of the time it has its perks. I know all
the murky details, and I have all the skeleton keys
to all the closets, and every one of them works.

You can find me at the bar, wearing my club jacket,
and I never drink alone. I'm the freaking Al Capone
in charge of investigating the misdeeds of myself.
I give a sweet caress to the hyoid bone of Elliott Ness.
I used to dine with Jeff Epstein and still spit-shine
frumpy old Billy Barr's valise and sole-less Weejuns.

Sometimes I break out the Ouija board to chat up
Mussolini, and sometimes, over a very dry martini,
we toast Mother Pence and break a crostini into
communion-size bits in remembrance of Scalia. Sure,
I aspire to the cosmopolitan pages of <u>Esquire</u>, like
Beto, but wind up in <u>The Inquirer</u> instead. Alas, alak!
Poor Yorick. I'll go to my squeaky Procrustean bed
with tee-time with the Taliban dancing in my head.

A man in my position might be called a martinet,
but I assure you, I am held in high trust, guarding
both the scepter and the flashy family jewels, rooting
through the waste, hurling prophets from the parapets.
A man in my position, a penny in the pocket of the throne,
sees the carefully choreographed musical chairs here, all
serving at the ruling sovereign's whim or as we say, pleasure,
arranging themselves in mad shapes to escape the jesters'
bullets enacted daily in the Star Chamber where the curtain falls
and they scamper and scurry into their hidey-holes in the wall.

You don't know me, but I pay the hush money and the blood money
to the laundress removing all the stains from the Emperor's new clothes.

# Silent Space

Photgraphy by Olivia Djawoto

Poetry by Louise Moises

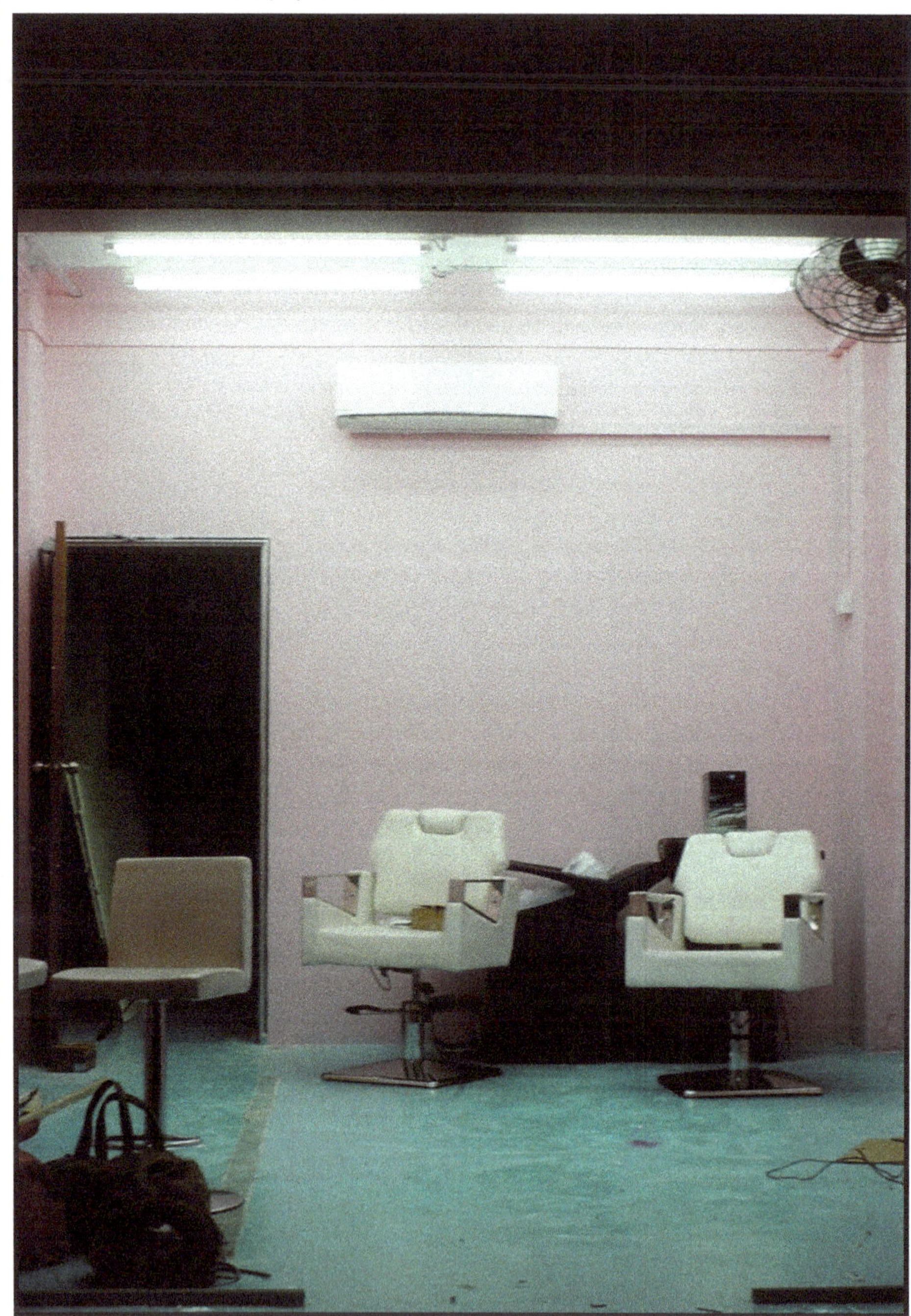

Empty chairs    silent space

fan no longer whirs    afraid to circulate the air

within pink walls    hovers dread

blinding neon only    evidence of occupation

a switch left on    by mistake

blue floor vacant    of clips of hair,

of fingernails,    carelessly swept

remnant of dust    spiraled cords

bag of tools    abandoned

when they fled in fear of the virus

        their clients had spread.

# In Order Of Appearance:

Joseph Zenoni is a poet living and working in Seattle. He calls all the best cities of the Midwest home.

Valyntina Grenier makes art on the side of life that insists, "Don't Shoot." Her poetry and visual art push the boundaries of representation and abstraction to create a vantage from which to view violence and prejudice. Her work has appeared or is forthcoming in, Lana Turner, JuxtaProse, Cathexis North West Press, Bat City Review, The Volta's Arroyo Chico and Spiral Orb. Her first chapbook Fever Dream/ Take Heart (a double) was released in January 2020 from Cathexis North West Press. Find her at valyntinagrenier.com or Insta @valyntinagrenier

Sara McCall is a writer living in Chicago, Il. She is 5'7".

April Rubasch received her MFA in creative writing with an emphasis in poetry from the University of Arizona in 2005. She was the recipient of the Fred N. Scott Award for fiction and the M.P. Hamilton Award for poetry through the University of Arizona in 2002 and was nominated for the 2004 Ruth Lily Poetry Fellowship Award. Her poem Snafu was published in Into the Teeth of the Wind in 2008. She recently received an "honorable mention" in Writer's Digest for her short story Snow.

V. B. Borjen was born in 1987 in the Socialist Republic of Bosnia and Herzegovina, Yugoslavia and now lives in the Czech Republic. His work in Bosnian has previously appeared in magazines across the former Yugoslav region and Hungary, including Strane, P.U.L.S.E., Symposion and B&H's oldest daily, Oslobodenje. His first poetry collection Prirucnik za levitiranje - Levitation Manual - won the 2012 Mak Dizdar Award and was published the following year to significant acclaim. His poetry and prose originally written in English have previously appeared in Hypothetical: A Review of Everything Imaginable, AZURE and The Esthetic Apostle. His paintings have been featured in Not Your Mother's Breast Milk, The Esthetic Apostle and Chaleur Magazine, while his photography is forthcoming in the January 2020 issue of Honey and Lime.

Katherine Lutz holds a B.A. in Biology and Spanish from Wellesley College and a M.S. in Science Journalism from Boston University. She is a longtime, Boston-based science and health writer and a more recent poet.

Bruce J. Berger received his MFA from American University in Washington, DC, and teaches College Writing and Creative Writing there now. His poem "Genesis" was previously published by High Shelf Press, and his other poetry has been published in a variety of literary journals.

Andrew Hutto writes out of Louisville, KY. He was recently awarded third place in the 2020 Flo Gault Poetry Prize. In the summer of 2019, he served as a preliminary judge for the Louisville Literary Arts Writer's Block fiction prize. Presently he serves on the Pine Row Press editorial board. His work appears or is forthcoming in Thrush Poetry Journal, Eunoia Review, Plum Tree Tavern, Amethyst Review, The Weekly Degree, Barnhouse Journal, After the Pause, and Math Magazine.

Jeff Scott Lane has a BFA in the study of Graphic Design from for Virginia Commonwealth University. He has mostly worked in bookstores but spends his free time still dedicated to his art be in in the form of writing, photography, music, block printing, video, or what ever medium best suits the project. Portfolio: www.VoicesDrownedByHelvetica.com

Tim Stiles lives and writes in the San Francisco-Bay Area. He received his MFA in Creative Writing from San Francisco State University. His poems, stories and lyrics have been published/recorded throughout the USA and Great Britain. His poetry-photography collaboration with photographer Jay Tyrrell, entitled Botmerica: Repeat After Me, was published in 2016.

Sara Dallmayr is originally from Kalamazoo, Michigan. She attended Western Michigan University and received a BA in English/creative writing/poetry. Her work has been published in The Esthetic Apostle, Texas Literary Review, The Tiny Seed Literary Journal, The Write Launch, and Glowworm. Dallmayr currently live in South Bend, Indiana, with her husband and three cats. She works for the post office as a rural carrier and sometimes prefers to slip into a dimension more comfortable.

Leon is an avid reader and aspiring writer of poetry. He has published in the Raw Art Review, Prometheus Dreaming Rumble Fish Quarterly and Cathexis Northwest Press. Leon has a book of poetry, The Uninvented Ear, coming out with UnCollected Press.

Christy Wisc is a poet, author, essayist and education equity activist. She is a student at Sierra Nevada's low-residency MFA program where she was awarded the Exceptional Manuscript scholarship. Her poems have appeared in Evening Street Press, Anthem, The Raven's Perch and NEBO Literary Journal. Wise divides her time between California and Washington DC.

Aaron Lelito is a visual artist from Buffalo, NY. In his photography and digital art, he is primarily drawn to the patterns and imagery of nature. Consequently, transformation is one of the reoccurring themes that he engages with--the changing of seasons, the flowing motion along a stream's bank, the waves breaking on Lake Erie's shoreline. There is creative potential embedded in images themselves, not only in the narrative sense of "telling a story," but in their ability to express the potential sights that often lay dormant in our everyday surroundings, a vision of what remains unseen by a passing view. Naturalist and writer Henry David Throeau emphasizes this renewed sense of vision and exploration that is embedded within the world around us: "Nature will bear the closes inspection; she invites us to lay our eye level with the smallest leaf and take an insect view of its plain. She has not interstices; every part is full of life." There is inspiration to be found in the seemingly ordinary—the more one looks, the more there is to see.

Corbin Wamble is a writer from Delaware.

Alec Montalvo is an emerging poet. His work has appeared in Cathexis Northwest Press, The Esthetic Apostle, and featured on the home page of PoetrySoup.com. He lives in Staten Island, New York, where the stars don't shine. Talk poetry with him on his Instagram @AlecInTheInk

Kateland Leveillee has been writing from a young age. She spent her life moving around the world. Her poetry can be found in literary magazines, online publications, and- perhaps most comprehensively- her living room trash can.

George L Stein is a writer and photographer in the New Jersey/New York metropolitan area. Interest in monochrome, film photography and urban decay/architectural subject matter has come to include street photography, fashion, fetish, collage, and oppositiional/juxtapositional projects in digital format. His work has been published in Midwest Gothic, NUNUM, Montana Mouthful, Out/Cast, The Fredericksburg Literary and Art Review, and DarkSide magazine.

Mark Reasoner is a Hoosier by birth, a teacher by profession and a storyteller by nature. He has previously published three novels and several short stories. He lives and writes in Neptune Beach, Florida.

John is a CPA who received an MBA (that's not a typo, an MBA) from Vanderbilt University, is now approaching retirement, and is both happy to finally be getting his stories out of his head and onto paper, and desperately hoping some kind soul will explain to him exactly what a run-on sentence is.

Joe Hedges is an intermedia artist who has developed an expansive practice that weaves together digital imaging, oil painting, new media, sound and installation. His projects often explore the effects of digital technologies on human experience. Hedges has exhibited nationally and internationally and is currently living in Pullman, Washington.

Jennifer Dines is a teacher in the Boston Public Schools and a mother of three daughters. Jennifer has been recognized by the US Department of Education, the Bill and Melinda Gates Foundation, Lady Gaga and the Born This Way Foundation, the World Literacy Organization, and the National Board for Professional Teaching Standards for her work with her students. She has struggled since her teens with depression, anxiety, bipolar disorder, alcohol abuse, and post-traumatic stress disorder. Jennifer enjoys cooking, pilates, reading, and especially watching her young daughters' growth in both creative and academic skills. She has been married to David Dines for fourteen years. More of her writing can be found here: https://literacychange.org/writing-portfolio/

Ed Scherrer lives in Toronto where malevolent forces beyond his control wreak havoc on his career.

Pamela Sumners is a constitutional and civil rights lawyer from Alabama. In 2018 and 2019, her work has been recognized or published by about 30 journals in the US, UK, Scotland, Ireland, and Singapore. She was selected for 2018's 64 Best Poets (Halcyone/Black Mountain Press) and was a 2018 Pushcart nominee. She is a member of the American Academy of Poets. She now lives in St. Louis with her wife, their son, and three rescue hounds.

Olivia revels in anachronisms—of shooting film in the 2000s; of writing fiction in the age of viral videos. Her interest in space is translated into a photography that seeks out light and void, absence and inertia, particularly in a world that can often be crowded in its own chaos.

Louise Moises was born and raised in San Francisco Bay Area, graduating from San Jose State with a major in Speech and Drama and minor in English. Over her seventy-five years she has been a teacher, a storyteller, a puppeteer, a retail clerk, and the owner of an antiquarian bookstore, along with being a wife, mother and grandmother. Now widowed, she enjoys traveling in her 23 foot RV with her cat, exploring places that inspire her writing. Her poems and stories have been recognized by the literary divisions of the San Mateo County and Marin County Fairs, the Ina Coolbrith Circle, Artists Embassy International, Bay Area Poets Coalition & Keats Soul Making, thewritelaunch and Unlimited Literature.

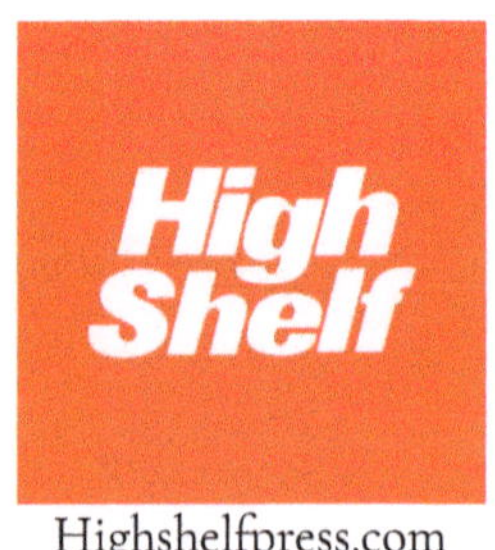


Highshelfpress.com